T0288042

ACKNOWLEDGEMENTS

I have long believed that my father's extraordinary life and achievements, not least being widely acclaimed as 'The Father of Education' in Syria, were a lesson to future generations. What is not written down is forgotten, and I felt this story worth telling.

My thanks go to all who contributed to the creation and publication of this book.

Compiling this book was not an easy task as many of my father's papers had been scattered. I would like to thank, in particular, Dr Sabah Kabbani, the author of this book. His meticulous research took him to the archives in France and Turkey, the Library of Congress and those of the Damascus University. Dr Kabbani succeeded in writing this as a novel rather than a traditional biography.

I would also like to thank Peter Clark, who has done a tremendous job of translating the manuscript from the original Arabic into English. His translation will enable my father's grandchildren and great-grandchildren and indeed many others to read this book in English.

My grateful thanks also go to Alice Dugdale, who, among many other things, worked diligently to help me find and select the wonderful photographs contained in this book.

Last, but not least, I would like to thank my nephew Ragheb Mudarres, who has contributed so much time and effort to this project. I cannot thank him enough for his many hours of impressive research, not least in compiling the family tree which was a most challenging task. I also thank him for overseeing the book's production and for encouraging those who have worked on it.

All these labours have created a fine story and an important historical record which I hope will be a source of inspiration to many.

Wafic Rida Saïd
February, 2021

RIDA SAÏD

A Man for All Seasons

Sabah Kabbani

Translated by Peter Clark

Published in 2021 by
HAUS PUBLISHING LTD
4 Cinnamon Row
London SW11 3TW

Originally published in Arabic as *Rida Sa'id: mu'assis al-jami'a
al-Suriya – rajul li-kull al-aqdar* by Sabah Kabbani
This edition published in agreement with Wafic Rida Saïd
English translation Copyright © 2021 Peter Clark

A CIP catalogue record for this book is available from the British Library

Typeset in Garamond by MacGuru Ltd

Printed in the UK by TJ Books

With acknowledgement to my friend, the
writer Yasir al-Malih, for reviewing these
pages before they were sent to press.

Dedicated to
WAFIC RIDA SAÏD
In appreciation of his initiative in taking over
the production of this book about the life of his
father – one of the most important builders of the
scientific and social renaissance in modern Syria.

CONTENTS

1

THE AWAKENING

The stories of all good books are truer than if they had
really happened.

Ernest Hemingway

Monday, 5 May 1913

Istanbul once again!

He left Taksim Square and headed towards the main
street of Beyoğlu, where he and his colleagues at the Medical
School used to go in their free time. Whencver they had any spare time from the toils of their
studies they would melt into this fine street flanked on both
sides by elegant shops, by entrances to covered malls with
their ornate ceilings, by the embassies of countries accredited
to the Sublime Porte with their imposing metal gateways
surmounted by fluttering national flags.

In the middle of the street swayed the one-carriage

tramway that slowly covered the short distance of the street, up and down, so slowly that passengers were able to exchange greetings with pedestrians and to wave cheerfully to people they knew or did not know among the crowds as they drifted along the pavements.

It was Istanbul once again: with its long streets, its magical coastline, its green hills, its mosques with their ash-coloured domes and tall, slender minarets reaching up to the heavens.

But was this really the Istanbul that he had known earlier, where he had spent his youth and early manhood? He wondered: What has changed here? Or was it he who had changed? Had the ugly Balkan war[1] changed him now he was returning from the war zone, worn out by the soldiers' wounds that he and his fellow doctors had dealt with at the military field hospital at the front? They had done all in their power to save them and to relieve their intense sufferings with what they had left in drugs and pain-killers. Here he was, even after having spent weeks away from the battlefield, still tortured – his hearing, his very existence were filled with cries of the soldiers in the middle of the night as they writhed in pain, asking in broken, rattle-like tones: "Why are we here? Why are we fighting? For what are we dying?"

He continued on his way with hastened steps, his heart pierced, as if by a spear, by the questions of those soldiers and by many others that he kept asking himself but to which he found no answer.

In this mood he had come back to Beyoğlu without resisting a nostalgia for the happy days of his youth. Indeed he was hoping to find clear answers from his old Syrian teacher, Yuzbashi[2] Umar Lutfi Effendi.[3] Thirty years earlier this man had taught him French in the elementary section of the Rushdiya Military School in Damascus. At the request of his father he had given him private lessons so he would become fluent in the language. This made it easy for him later to study medicine in Istanbul and then in Paris. Umar Lutfi was his father's close friend. He regularly paid visits to his family in their fine house with its extensive garden in Bustan al-A'jam[4], the Persian Garden, overlooking the Al-Salimiya tekke and surrounded by the meadows on both sides of the Barada River.

Umar Lutfi was so proficient in French that the authorities sent him from the province of Damascus to Galatasaray School in Istanbul for two years, making use of his language and organisational skills after he had completed his military service. As well as his immersion in French he also had a wide general culture. His analytical mind was characterised by precision and objectivity, which he could articulate with an elegance that was appreciated by everyone who sat around him during intimate evening gatherings at their Damascus house.

He was now at the end of the principal road; on the left was the entrance to his old school. He went through the great gateway and strolled over to the garden with its tall trees and its water channels zigzagging among beds of flowers of many colours. He paused at the enquiries office to ask the official on duty to say he had come to call on Ustaz Umar Lutfi Effendi. The official stared at the visitor in smart military uniform. When he became aware of his rank, which was clear from his epaulette, he welcomed him with the words,

"*Kul ağası*⁵ Rida Saïd... if I am not mistaken?"

"Yes, that's me."

"The Ustaz will be waiting for you. His office is the third on the right in the courtyard facing you. Welcome back to Galatasaray."

As soon as he reached the room with the door open, Ustaz Umar Lutfi looked up from behind his desk and ran forward to greet his old student. He embraced him with open arms and clutched him to his chest, the embrace of a father for his son after a long separation.

"You are most welcome, most welcome. Rida. Excuse me for addressing you just by your name and not giving you the proper military salute," he added joyfully. "I am a yuzbashi on pension and you – *ma sha'Allah* – are a doctor of kulağa rank. Ah! How this rank suits you. I have not congratulated you for that yet! But being in civilian dress, as you see, my son, may mitigate the offence."

"Please, sir, you embarrass me. First and last, you will always be my esteemed teacher who smothered me with his kindness and his knowledge from my earliest years. I continue to be your pupil whatever my rank."

His teacher invited him to take a seat. He looked serious

on perceiving anxiety in the countenance and words of his pupil.

"I have always been concerned about you, ever since I learned from your worthy father, Miralai, General Muhammad Saïd, before I left Damascus at the end of last year, that you were on the front line in the Balkan War. Thanks be to God, the war is over and you have come back to us safe and sound."

"*Al-hamdu li'llah*, praise be to God. It's true that the military operations stopped in the middle of last month, but the impact of the war isn't over. We are still overcome with its concerns. Although the war lasted only six months, it's had a devastating effect on our army. According to our medical statistics, over a hundred thousand men are dead or wounded. Moreover we have lost most of our lands in Europe. Indeed the Balkan allies almost stormed Istanbul itself. All this becomes of no account in the face of the frightening collapse of morale among officers, men and civil ranks. This used to be a matter of glory and pride. It seems that the futility of war has ruined everything, and..."

At this point Umar Lutfi interrupted him.

"What about carrying on this conversation somewhere else?" he said. "I am free today to sit with you. There's a lot I'd like to know about your life since you left Damascus and pursued your studies and specialisation. I've learnt only a bit of your news from talking with your dear father. It would be nice if you could give me a few minutes to clear these papers in front of me. We can then set off for some quiet place nearby so I can offer you some coffee and sweetmeats."

Rida Saïd spent this time looking hard at his teacher as he worked. How much his features had changed since he had last seen him for a few minutes, ten years earlier, during a short leave he had in Damascus. Grey hair now covered his head, and wrinkles furrowed his face and neck. His hands had become emaciated. But his features had not changed at all, and had not been spoiled by the passing of years. His compassionate deep-lined eyes still sparkled with youth and intelligence. His genial voice gave out a sense of tranquillity and calmness to whoever listened to him.

An unusual calm reigned over the reception room of the Pera Palace Hotel. There were only a few people scattered around in comfortable leather armchairs, having conversations in barely audible tones. It was no longer a place bubbling with the buzz of activity, and filled with the bustle of travellers who had come from Europe on the Orient Express railway, arriving at the hotel in carriages that had transferred them from Sirkeci station. This hotel had been originally constructed to accommodate them. But the war had put a stop to railway travel, leading to the disappearance of those guests, creating a heavy calm that prevailed in the different areas and courtyards of the hotel.

The two men went to the bar and selected a secluded corner overlooking the broad hotel balcony, adorned with flowering plants. When they had settled down Ustaz Umar asked the waiter to bring two coffees and some sweetmeats.

"We can talk here," he said. "Where were we...? "

"I was telling you about this accursed war..."

The Ustaz interrupted him.

"Let's leave aside the war. We can talk about that later. Tell me about yourself and the splendid events in your life. Ah! I remember. I heard that you got married in Paris to a French girl. Congratulations to you both! I'll not hide the fact that I'm doubly happy. First about this happy event, and second, because the language that I made you perfect in when you were young has been useful to you when you were grown up, not just in your medical studies but also in matters of love and marriage. But where is your bride? And where are you living?"

"After we came to Istanbul, my wife and I rented a small flat with my wife's mother, who came with us from Paris. It was near the Military Medical School where I took up my old job as a teacher of ophthalmology. But when war broke out, on the evening before I left for the front, my elder brother, Dr Salih, and his wife insisted that Marcelle and her grandmother should not stay by themselves in the flat. They thought it was better that they move in with them until I came back from the front, especially as my wife was newly pregnant. But after I came back my brother insisted that we should all stay together in their large house overlooking the Bosphorus until my wife had to go to the maternity hospital for the birth due at the end of this or the beginning of next month."

"Anticipated congratulations for this happy event. Had I known that you were with your brother, dear Dr Salih, I'd have made contact with him before you took the initiative in contacting me.

"But do tell me about your work in the Military Medical School and about your progress in becoming a teacher at that important institution. I remember that you told me when we met briefly in Damascus ten years ago, just before you came back here after a short leave in Syria, that you had just graduated from the Military Medical School in Istanbul and that you were expecting to be appointed to a post there."

"You've got an amazing memory, sir!" Rida smiled. "It's still as brilliant as ever. We, your students at the Rushdiya Military School, we were impressed by your memory, and frightened of it at the same time; you knew everything, great or small, about us, each one of us."

He took a sip of coffee and went on.

"About two months after I qualified as a surgeon at the Military Medical School in September 1902, I was appointed as a doctor with the rank of yuzbashi in Istanbul. But one year later I was suddenly transferred to Trabzon, in Trebizond, to head the chemical section of the port customs administration. At first I was thrilled to go to that beautiful coastal city on the Black Sea, famed for its gorgeous gardens and its fruit – you know about this…"

At this point the Ustaz interrupted him, laughing,

"It is the fruit with a name that we in Damascus distorted. We called Trebizond dates, Darabzin dates, 'Banister' dates, as you know."

"You will also be amused when I tell you that I regarded going to Trebizond as a good sign because there is a town nearby with a name that is similar to mine – Rize. But my enthusiasm for the place soon faded away when it became clear to me that in the work to which I was assigned, in spite of its importance, I wasn't doing what I wanted to do and what I was competent to practise and to do well. Fortunately the chemical section was abolished entirely just four months after I arrived in Trebizond. I came back to Istanbul in April 1904 where I was appointed surgeon at Gulhane Hospital. It was not long before I became an assistant in the Department of Eye Surgery in the Military Medical School, where I had graduated only two years earlier. It seems that the hard work I had done there was appreciated by my professor, the celebrated General As'ad Pasha, for he asked me in 1907 to be his assistant in teaching ophthalmology in that school. Just one year later I was promoted to the rank of doctor kulağa, the rank you see that I now hold. I was then sent to Paris for two years to specialise in ophthalmology – that was from 1909 to 1911. I praise God that He helped me in all the stages which I went through. It was all due to God above and to the satisfaction, the *rida*, of my father."

"It is true that every man has the luck of his name," Ustaz Umar said. "Your noble father selected for you when you were born the name Rida, meaning satisfaction, and you were always cause for satisfaction, and he never stopped expecting satisfaction in everything you undertook. Whenever your name came up in company he would play on words with the traditional saying, 'May God be satisfied with you, Rida.' There is no doubt that he had a special place in his heart for you. I'm not saying that he preferred you above your dear brothers Salih and Munir, for you were all equal in his eyes, but his love for you was blended with a special tenderness because you never knew the tenderness of a mother, for he lost your mother, Lady Khadija, may Allah have mercy on her soul, when you were a baby, and at that time and for long afterwards, your father was overwhelmed with gloom by her death because it happened quite suddenly, a terrible tragic event. It changed the way he thought and it changed the course of his life."

At this, distress appeared on Rida's face. He put a sweetmeat that was in his hand back on to the plate.

"What are you saying, sir? This is something I haven't heard before. All I know is that I opened my eyes to the world but found that I had no mother. Tell me, please, how did she die? What was this tragic event that you speak of? And what is the story of the gloom that overcame my father? You, my dear Ustaz, were closer than anyone else to my family. Each one of us sees you as one of us. I am sure you know all the details."

Confronted with these anxious insistent questions, Ustaz Umar saw that he had to go on talking about what he knew of events that had taken place thirty-six years earlier, but it was as if it had happened yesterday. It could never be forgotten because of its strangeness and distressing finality.

"First of all, I apologise for mentioning this old story, for I assumed that you had already been told the painful details. I would not otherwise have let it slip my tongue and spoken of it. It's probable that your worthy father concealed it from you until such time when it would not disturb you or your studies. For him this was his first concern. I don't want now to conceal from you anything beyond what your father concealed from you.

"My dear Rida, you know that your father, General Muhammad Saïd, was one of the senior cavalry officers in the fifth division of the Fifth Ottoman Army; that was considered the most important army in the state. Damascus was chosen to be its base because of its geographical and spiritual importance. It was in the centre of Syria and was the gathering point for Syrian pilgrims when they set out for the Holy Places. Your father had had local administrative responsibility for the whole of southern Syria.

"The officers and men of the Fifth Army were noted for their fine qualities. They underwent constant rigorous military training, learning from the well-known methods of the German Army with its rigour and severity. The units of the fifth division carried out their military manoeuvres under the supervision of senior German officers in the desert.

"One day in January 1877 the Germans decided to carry out manoeuvres with the Ottoman Army with live ammunition. I remember that day well because it was very cold. There were violent icy storms that the people of Damascus had never known before. In spite of the tempestuous winter atmosphere, the German supervisors obstinately insisted on carrying out the manoeuvres as arranged, at dawn.

"Your mother, Lady Khadija, had complete faith in the courage and competence of her husband. But she was filled with anxiety as the hours went by. Night fell and he had not returned. You were not more than nine months old at the time. She settled you down and there were more moments of anxiety when your father's horse returned without its master. To the relief of the household the General arrived during the following morning.

"What had happened was that the stormy weather with its dreadfully heavy fall of snow had impaired visibility on the training ground, changing it to what seemed like a vast lake of thick mud. This paralysed the movement of horses and artillery. It led to delays in the plans for the manoeuvres and created chaos in the ranks of the combined units. Individuals became separated in the gloom of the dawn with no guidance or discipline. The horses seemed also to be disturbed and difficult to control. They were neighing crazily as they tried to extract themselves from the mud they had fallen into. The General had dismounted from his horse to concentrate on the cavalry units and get them all together, as did commanders of the other sections. When the feeble daylight began to pierce through on the training ground, it became possible, albeit with some difficulty, to work out the positions of individuals scattered far from their original location. They finally got back to their units, mechanically lined them up and extracted the horses from the mud they were stuck in.

"The unit commanders were now opposing the strange proposal of those German supervisors who wanted to get them all back to the manoeuvres. The commanders wanted to bring them back to the city. Of course you can imagine the enormous workload your father had in that stormy weather when he decided to return all sections of his unit to their barracks. But he was unable to come across his horse and he had to return to his house in a military vehicle.

"On his return from these most difficult manoeuvres, to his shock and horror, he learned from your father that his wife had died of sepsis. He was told that she had fallen ill during his absence and, although the doctor had attended on her, he had been unable to treat her fast enough to reduce her high fever. Your father was shattered by her death. Feeling completely lost, and separated from his family, he was unable to imagine how he would bring you up, a small baby, without your mother and with no family help."

Ustaz Umar paused in his narrative and saw that Rida's eyes were filled with tears. He tried to smile and continued with a forced liveliness,

"My dear Rida, I brought you here so we could refresh ourselves, not to get depressed. You have come from the field of battle, and I have come from my field of toil. Please wipe away your tears; the people here might wonder you really are an officer. Officers don't cry! Let's order some more fresh coffee and then we can carry on talking."

Rida wiped away the tears that were pouring down his cheek.

"You said that these events led to a great change in my father's life and in his way of thinking. I only know him as he is now, and as I have always known him, ever since I came into the world. What was it that changed in him?"

"He changed the way he looked at things entirely. He

discovered how he ought to behave in the future, whether it was in relation to his military work or with regard to the future of yourself."

"Myself?"

"Yes, Rida, because your beloved mother's death was in effect a turning point in both his professional and family life. He did not want to believe that she had left him, and for most of the time he remained silent, his eyes looking all over the place, unable to concentrate.

"For several months your father was beset with great distress. He recovered some of his self-control. The first thing he did was to go to the commander of the Fifth Army with a written request to be transferred from the cavalry division to a desk job so he could spend more time with you and your brothers, Salih and Munir.

"He took his family to Istanbul where, a few months later, recognising his talents and experience in the region, Sultan Abdul Hamid II appointed him Mutasarrif, or Governor, of the Hauran Province in the south of Syria. After that, your father never saw active military service again.

"As for your studies, from that time, he decided that he did not want you to be like him, simply an officer in the army who knew no profession outside the military. He was determined that you should have another career, another specialisation."

"But in my early childhood he enrolled me in the elementary section of the Rushdiya Military School in Damascus!"

"That's true. He had to do that. The Rushdiya Military

School was part of the programme of educational reform undertaken by the Ottoman state. These schools were the best at that time when compared with the available national schools. There were anyway only a few of them. He intended you to have a good grounding and then study in Istanbul and join the preparatory section of the Military Medical School. This grounding included, in addition to the ordinary studies in the Rushdiya Military School was, where most subjects were taught in Turkish, a concentration on perfecting Arabic, your mother tongue. He arranged for you to have private lessons with a skilled teacher, our colleague Lieutenant Abdul Rahman. It was my good fortune that your honoured father selected me at this time to help you become proficient in French.

"Your father realised early that it was a mistake to embark on educational reform solely out of military considerations after the pressure of the tempestuous events that the Ottoman state had faced since the beginning of the last century. He believed that the most important endeavour in educational and cultural development was that undertaken by the previous Grand Vizier, Midhat Pasha, when he was Wali of Damascus in 1878 – you were then just two years old. He encouraged the setting up of schools and cultural and social societies (such as the Maqasid Charitable Society in Beirut). He started to collect books for the public library, Dar al-Kutub. He encouraged the fine arts, such as drama and music, to take the place of the shadow puppets (the *karagöz*) with its debased language and uncouth expressions.

It distressed him that they were the only diversion of the people of Damascus. Your father told me that Midhat Pasha summoned a youth who wanted passionately to improve his composition of music and drama – his name was Ahmad al-Kabbani. He had heard about him and his theatrical narratives derived from traditional tales. They had only been put on for some of his friends in their houses. But Midhat Pasha asked him to present these dramas in some public place. He granted him 900 gold pounds to spend on scenery and costumes required for performing these dramas in the proper way. In order to win the people of Damascus over to this fine art form, he invited the notables of the city, the sheikhs and senior army officers, among whom was Governor Muhammad Saïd, to see the first musical theatre production written by al-Kabbani. Midhat Pasha collected his poems and songs and had them published."

"Yes, I remember my father telling me that just before I went to Trebizond, when news reached him of the death of Ahmad Abu Khalil al-Kabbani in 1903, after a life full of theatre and music in Egypt and Syria. He was much distressed at his death. He was always expressing his appreciation of the fine artistic work he used to follow in Damascus. He never forgot that night when he received an invitation from the Wali, Midhat Pasha, to see the play 'Shah Mahmud' in Khan Jumruk."

"Unfortunately the waliship of Midhat Pasha lasted less than two years. But your father was inspired with the new spirit released in the province of Syria by the great Wali. He continued with his own project of bringing you up with a rounded culture – in medicine, languages and the arts. He had no hesitation in sending you to Istanbul in 1888 in spite of your youth, for you were then not more than twelve years old. You were sent to pursue studies in the preparatory section attached to the Military Medical School. That meant that he was unable to have you at his side."

"...Yes, it's true what you say. I remember that whenever I came to Damascus on vacation, my father insisted that I continue to be exposed to all kinds of information and not to concentrate solely on medical studies. So shortly before I went off to Paris for specialist medical studies, he advised me that whenever I had the chance, I should go to the theatre and concerts, and attend art exhibitions. I should read new books so I could become familiar with intellectual currents prevailing there. I followed his advice for all the time I was in France."

"Yes, he wanted you to be a doctor steeped in a wide culture so that you could return and benefit your homeland with your knowledge and expertise and..."

"Excuse me if I interrupt you here. I pause for a moment, sir, at the word *homeland*. In all his letters he always took care to repeat the phrase *return to the homeland*. When he wrote this I felt that he was hinting rather than being explicit... I only came to you today to clear up a number of issues that were on my mind and were perplexing me. Among these was that expression. I was never able to talk to my father about what homeland he meant... Was it when the Ottoman flag fluttered over Serbia, Bulgaria and Montenegro and the rest of the European territories, where we have been waging a bloody war for six months against those Balkan states allied against us? Or was the homeland Istanbul that has, for us and our fathers and grandfathers, been a symbol of the Islamic Caliphate and our extensive Ottoman Empire? Or was it for my father *bilad al-Sham*, the land of Greater Syria, that he never ever left and where he and his forebears were born, and where I myself was born and reared under his care?"

"This has not only confused you, my son, it has confused us all. The events of the last few years have made each one of us, and especially officers like us, ask ourselves the same questions. You have wrestled with the same questions. After you returned to Istanbul from the front you wanted relief from your anger and from the distress about the tragedies affecting thousands of souls who have been sacrificed in this futile, avoidable war. That is why I brought you here, to this quiet, isolated place, far from eyes and ears.

"As for your wondering about what your father meant by *homeland*, I would say that we are all people of bilad al-Sham; but for hundreds of years we have known another homeland and that is the land of the Ottoman state; we have known only one allegiance and that is an allegiance to its identity. General Muhammad Saïd knew that he and all the officers in the province of Syria were the most comfortable class, and during the reign of Sultan Abdul Hamid they obtained many privileges, in pay, promotion and allowances and so on. But all these privileges never distracted your father from an objective view on issues. They did not make him forget the deteriorating condition of the Syrian community or the gross neglect from which the city of Damascus suffered. This was the most important and the biggest city in bilad al-Sham, as far as education, culture and health were concerned.

"We imagined that the deposition of Sultan Abdul Hamid which the Committee of Union and Progress effected four years ago would make matters better. But everything became worse, both internally and externally. Unexpectedly, as you know, a new and hateful refrain began to talk about 'Arabs' and 'Turks.' This was a racial distinction that had not been known before. We only knew that we, all of us, were Ottomans. We rallied to an imperial standard as one force. Turks and Arabs, who were equal in number, composed three-quarters of the Ottoman nation. Many Arabs were only demanding the implementation of the slogan of 'equality,' which the Unionists had professed during their revolution in 1908. They also demanded that the Arabs be granted their national rights in sharing in the governance of the Ottoman state, with the recognition of Arabic as an official language in the Arab provinces. But soon the tone of the Unionists changed from dislike of the Arab element to contempt of Arabs and a sense of superiority over them. Indeed they openly assumed the worst of them."

"Yes, I remember my colleague, Ahmad Qadri, who, like me, studied medicine in Paris. He told me, when we met up there, that he saw in Istanbul shortly after the revolution one of the Unionist officers – his name was Sirri Bey – addressing a group of people. He heard him cursing Arabs and describing them as traitors. Indeed some of the newspapers of the capital – in particular *Iqdam* – used to refer to 'flithy Arabs.' It made the Arabs living in Istanbul – writers, officials, graduates of the higher institutes – shudder. They were angry and convened meetings where they protested against these expressions. They chose one of them, our friend Abdul Qadir al-Azm, a graduate of the Maliki School, to make a note of this objection and send it to the authorities.

"My colleague Ahmad Qadri told me in confidence that he and some of his friends had made up their minds to make a move to defend their Arab stock. They set up secret societies that aimed to stop the racist campaign against Arabs, and to demand reforms in the Ottoman state that would ensure their rights and establish a decentralised administration in each Arab province.

"When my colleague sensed that I was in sympathy with these demands and with their efforts, he wanted me to conceal what was going on and not to reveal any activity so as not to prejudice my medical career or risk the cancellation of my being sent officially to France to pursue my specialisation. He mentioned that he had many colleagues taking part in this political work and that they were scattered – in Istanbul, in Paris, in Beirut and in Cairo. He preferred at this juncture that I save myself for the future. Nobody knew how things would develop, and, he added, 'God may want to take us by the hand; we must help one another, all of us, civilians, army officers and especially medical officers from Syria, who have nothing to do with those racists.'"

At this point Ustaz Umar spoke.

"From this I imagine that there is something of this kind in your father's mind when he spoke to you about the homeland. He was one of the first to realise the dimensions of the Arab–Turkish struggle because, as you know, he retired from the army three years ago, that is, less than a year after the revolution, and he started to see, with new eyes, evidence of that struggle in the dismissal and transfer of a large number of his Arab fellow officers because they were under suspicion. Some of those officers had expressed their scornful disapproval of the Unionists in their defence of another Arab province, that is to say, Libya, when Italy invaded. They accused them of withdrawing the Turkish troops from there with the aim of sending them to fight Arabs in Yemen and Asir instead of against the Italians.

"What most kept the General awake at night was the growing burden of foreign concessions, the scope of which extended in proportion as the Ottoman monarchy became weaker and weaker in the face of European forces, especially Russia, France, Britain and Italy, who were all waiting for any possible opportunity to gobble up a bit of the Empire. It was not long before Germany also joined the race for influence. Germany entered the field of organising and training the Ottoman Army, as well as building railways. This German penetration reached its zenith, it will be recalled, when Kaiser Wilhelm II and his wife came to Damascus in 1898. The Kaiser gave a speech in which he counted himself as a sincere friend and lover of Islam and of Muslims!

"Your father became especially sensitive to – indeed pessimistic about – the increase in German influence after the arrival of the Unionists. German domination grew in Istanbul in political and military matters. He realised that the German initiatives were not inspired by sympathy and affection, as the Kaiser claimed that day, but at extending the strategic interests of Germany at the expense of British interests and at attempting to take over the lines of communication between Britain and India.

"Shortly before I set out for Istanbul, I met your father and he made it clear to me that he was pessimistic about the increase in the influence the Germans wielded over the Unionists; indeed he mentioned the background of the increasing economic and military rivalry among the European states and their ill-considered arms race. He was concerned about the bellicose statements issued by the German high command in which they expressed their belief in the inevitability of a European war and that victory would be their ally.

"The General pointed out that, in the context of this frenetic European atmosphere, the Germans might, by claiming friendship with us, be aiming to draw us to their side in any probable conflict. They talked about it openly. Only God knew what would be the fate of our state at the end of the day."

"But didn't the authorities learn a lesson from the horrendous crisis of the Balkan War that has almost destroyed the whole state?"

"This war, my dear Rida, did not come suddenly or out of nowhere. The Balkan states have for a long time, from the time of Sultan Abdul Hamid, been asking Istanbul for administrative decentralisation, similar to what Arabs are now demanding. But there was no response. These provinces expected the Unionists – who had adopted the slogans of the French Revolution (Liberty, Fraternity, Equality) – to respond to their demands, but they failed to do so. We doubtless remember the Foreign Minister of Austria-Hungary, Count Berchtold, already knew of the alliance that Bulgaria, Serbia, Montenegro and Greece were preparing under the sponsorship of Russia, against the Ottoman state. He advised the authorities in Istanbul to respond to the demands of Balkan provinces and give them some of the administrative decentralisation they were demanding. But they were slow to take his advice. And so there was war.

"Perhaps you heard what the French newspaper *Le Temps* wrote about this? It reported that when Abdul Hamid, in exile in Anatolia, heard about the alliance of the Balkan states and the war, he said, 'Wow! How did they let these states agree with each other? For thirty-three years I was working to spread dissension among them!'"

Suddenly both men simultaneously took out their pocket watches to see the time. They both laughed together. They noticed that time had passed and that their talk had taken unexpected turns. It had toured the horizons of the distant past and the near present. They did not know how these three hours, ranging between the past and the present, had flown without them realising it.

"I don't know how to thank you, sir, for all you have told me. You have enlightened me about much that has been obscure to me. I only came to see you to get some relief for what had been troubling me," said Rida to his teacher as they were preparing to leave the hotel lounge.

"You too deserve thanks, Rida. You enabled me to expand on what has been on my mind. I didn't think I could talk about these things to anyone here before. Anyway I hope we can meet again, but don't forget to tell me when you become a father so I can come and offer you my congratulations. That will be soon, inn sha'Allah."

Sunday, 15 June 1913

The concerns of Ustaz Umar Lutfi Effendi at the school only allowed him to call on Rida two weeks after the arrival of his eldest son, Adnan, who was born on 1 June. When he called on him at the house of Dr Salih Saïd in Büyükdere, a village overlooking the Bosphorus, he was greeted by Rida and his two brothers, Salih and Munir, who were both living in Istanbul, and other members of the family. Ustaz Umar knew most of them from having met them in Damascus at the house of General Muhammad Saïd. After offering his congratulations on the happy event, they all sat and chatted. Then Ustaz Umar expressed a wish to see Adnan. The mother brought him in. At first the Ustaz did not notice that the person who came in was Rida's French wife. It seemed to him that she was an Eastern woman with an ornamental head-dress covering her hair and a transparent white yashmak that covered half her face, allowing only her eyes to be seen. When she welcomed him in French he realised that she was Adnan's mother. He congratulated her and Rida and gave a present for the bonny newborn babe.

She then said to him, "My husband has spoken a lot about you. I have been looking forward to meeting his esteemed teacher. I now know from where your dear student learnt his perfect French accent."

"And I in my turn, Madame, can see how you have obtained from Dr Rida and from the excellent Saïd family this Eastern taste in your dress."

"But my husband tells me that a different fashion waits for me in Damascus when I go there shortly. I know that most orientalists, men and women, who live in the East wear the clothes of the people they live among. The British artist John Frederick Lewis adopted the dress of Egypt, and the English lady, Jane Digby used to wear Bedu dress after she married the Bedu Majwal al-Musrab and lived with him at Palmyra. Indeed my fellow Frenchwoman Isabelle Eberhardt who lived in Algeria, where she embraced Islam, used to wear men's dress there and adopted the name Si Mahmud. And what about Damascene dress? My husband tells me I may be obliged to cover my body with a cloak, a *mala'a*, and my face with a flimsy dark coloured veil, a *niqab*. Is this what it would be appropriate for me to wear?"

"What the appropriate dress to wear in Damascus is," replied Ustaz Umar, "depends on your personal judgement. It varies according to the quarter in which you will live. I know that even today there are a number of respectable Christian families resident in the Midan quarter who are conservative, for example, their women still dressing the same as Muslim women. Among these families are the families of Farah, Ghanajah, Sabbagh, Abu Hadid, al-Khuri, al-Dumani, al-Shuwairi and many others."

Those present confirmed what Ustaz Umar said, adding that they knew all these families referred to, and that when they saw a group of women in the street, they were unable to tell whether they were Christian or Muslim.

"I would also like to make clear, Madame," added Ustaz Umar, "that the covering of the face for us is of Byzantine origin, and Muslim women only adopted it after the conquest of Syria in the seventh century, with the aim of following the practice of elite Byzantine women in the Syrian community."

Then Madame Marcelle said, her voice full of happiness, "in that case I shall follow this practice as soon as I arrive in Syria."

She thanked Ustaz Umar for his visit, and for the lovely gift, and for his useful explanation. She said goodbye to him and turned to go to the back of the house, carrying her infant.

Then Ustaz Umar asked Rida, "Is it true, what I have heard, that you are shortly going to Damascus?"

"Yes, this is something I was wanting to tell you. After we parted a fortnight ago, the authorities told me that the military hospital in Damascus, currently under construction, needs a large group of military doctors, and that General Ahmad Nadir Bey, who will be the head of this team, has called for doctors, recruiting them from among those still in Istanbul. They will proceed to Damascus and be the first medical team in charge in the new military hospital. They may alternate with a number of my Syrian fellow doctors. In my capacity as the most senior in rank, I have encouraged them to join up. My colleagues have all agreed and we informed the authorities what had been decided. Indeed the decree has been issued transferring me and my fellow doctors to Damascus. They are Ahmad Ratib, Tahir al-Jaza'iri, Abdul Qadir Sirri, Satraki Chan, as well as a group of other Ottoman doctors."

"I'm so delighted to hear this news! Because we shall shortly meet up in Damascus. My assignment to Istanbul will terminate at the end of the summer."

Ustaz Umar then said, with apologies, that he had to leave and go back to the school. He got up and said his farewells to everybody. Rida left with him to escort him to the garden gate.

"The time, then, for your going to Damascus draws near, Rida."

"Say rather, to repeat the expression my father used in his letters, the time draws near for *the return to the homeland*."

2

FORMATION

The evening train for Damascus was two whole hours late in setting off from Aleppo station. But Dr Rida Saïd, in spite of his long, anxious wait with his two small children and their great-grandmother, preferred not to leave their seats in the compartment to which they had been led by the uniformed railway official. This man had suddenly appeared from among the crowd of passengers. He made a way for them with great solicitude and some difficulty through the chaotic press of the crowds that were cramming the station halls and the departure platforms.

There was limited seating but that gallant official had found places for them, but it meant that when they took their children and left the train to get a breath of fresh air, they may not find the seats unoccupied when they returned. They would then have to split up, going to different compartments on the train or to remain, as best as they could, in one carriage but standing in the corridor, crammed with others for the whole journey. This was unimaginable with two small children. Adnan was not yet six years old, and Rafic was no more than twenty months. They would not reach Damascus, after going via Hama, Homs and Riyaq, until after thirty hours. In those days the train travelled very slowly because the fuel was wood, taken from five million trees and then chopped into millions of small pieces. There was then a dearth of the coal used for trains. Along with other commodities coal had run out during the war years, which had been years of hunger, desperation and disease in the land of Syria.

Priority in getting on the train had been given to officers and soldiers of the Arab Army who had been trickling back in groups to Aleppo station, and who were soon filling the coaches to take them back to Damascus after they had chased the remnants of the Turkish Army after its collapse and as it was in retreat heading towards Anatolia.

Before the guard gave the signal to the driver to set off, the official decided to reassure those to whom he had extended a helping hand. He ran to the coach where he had seated them. When he was alongside the compartment, he looked through the window and saw the head of the family with lowered head and deep in thought, regardless of the turmoil that was going on around him. But when he heard the guard tapping on the window, he looked up, got up and opened the window. Struggling with a smile, he greeted him, wanting to thank him, but the official interrupted him, speaking rapidly and disjointedly.

"Dr Rida Saïd, I have just come here to reassure you.

Perhaps you may not remember me, sir. Shortly before the war I worked with the doctors on the Hijaz Railway; I worked with you when you were the boss. I'll never forget the care you took of all your staff, senior and junior. I'll always remember that you helped me by getting me transferred here so I could be with my family in Aleppo. And when today I spotted you from afar among dozens of people as they thronged into the station, I realised that you were my kind old boss. I came to see if I could help you and those with you to get through this swarm of people, this chaos for which I apologise. But it's the war, as you know, sir! The trains, they are few, and slow."

"Thank you, thank you, my son, for all your help and consideration, and for getting us some good seats in difficult circumstances. But tell me, Mr..."

"Mahmud."

"Tell me, Mr Mahmud, when do we depart?"

"Immediately, sir. Allow me then to say farewell. I must go and tell the driver that the train must move. Have a good journey. May God protect you!"

A few minutes later the engine blew its whistle and belched out thick black smoke that covered all parts of the station and everyone there. Smoke penetrated the doors and open windows of the carriages, reached the chests of the passengers and brought tears to their eyes. They rubbed their eyes to offset the sting brought on by the wood smoke from the engine boiler.

❧

The train was now on the move...

Also on the move in Rida's mind were memories of events, sweet and bitter, that had filled his life and the lives of those whose destinies were linked to his.

Once the train had left the city and was picking up speed, Dr Rida sat down and looked thoughtfully through the window, seeing trees and telegraph poles alongside the railway line and slipping back as they advanced. Images of his life, likewise, followed in succession, slipping into the background, one image after another, rhythmically like the passing of those trees, one after another.

In this year he became forty-two years of age. But he felt that the events that his life had witnessed were enough, in number, intensity and impact, to be spread over two hundred years.

Within three months after his day of birth, two Ottoman sultans were deposed and a third installed. This was Abdul Hamid, who knew how to hold on to his throne for thirty-three years, years that were the beginning of the end of the Ottoman state, the disintegration of which was mirrored in himself, on his view of the world and on the course of his life.

Rida was an infant when his mother had died, and during the years of his youth and his manhood, he missed the love of a mother about whom he heard but whom he never knew. His sense of loss increased when, at the age of twelve, he found himself alone in Istanbul, where his father had sent him for his studies, far from his place of birth and the care of his father.

There, at that early age, he realised that his father wanted him to be a man before he had reached the age of manhood. From that time there was always a sadness haunting his eyes. He concentrated on his studies and excelled in them. He was the outstanding student at all stages, and did supremely well in all important tasks with which he was entrusted after he graduated from the Colleges of Medicine in both Istanbul and Paris. This constant appreciation for his capabilities for some time pleased him, but his pleasure was destroyed by dark events that overwhelmed him, coming from he knew not where. His short-term glory was always accompanied by a sadness that kept returning to his life again and again, and stayed with him for a very long time.

The engine whistled and Rafic stirred at its scream. He opened his eyes, then soon closed them again and returned to his sleep; he was being cuddled by his great-grandmother who smothered him with care and tender warmth. Adnan was sitting, huddled up beside his father, sunk in a deep sleep. He was rocked by the rhythmic wheels of the train.

Rida looked up to the face of the boys' great-grandmother, and saw the concern and distress that was also affecting him. He was alarmed at the way the faint yellow light coming from a lamp on the ceiling of the compartment would become fainter, would flicker and seem to contract. But for the silent tears that trickled down her cheeks, the observer would consider that her face was of wax, untouched by life.

Ah! How much had the features on this kindly face changed since first he saw it in Paris just nine years earlier. How much these features reflected concern and worry, as a result of unanticipated events.

When Rida arrived in Paris on the last day of May 1909, he chose to reside in the fifth arrondissement, in the heart of the Latin Quarter, with its famous French cultural institutions about which he had heard and read: the Sorbonne, Le Collège de France and the Panthéon, the College of Medicine and the College of Law, the Odéon theatre, the libraries, the coffee-houses whose tables inside and on the pavements were the meeting places of writers, poets, students and lawyers.

He wanted to live in the atmosphere of this quarter and to fill his heart and soul with the aura of the deep culture in which it was steeped. At the same time he wanted to be near his place of work at the Hôtel-Dieu Hospital where he would be completing his specialisation. So he was delighted when he came across a comfortable apartment on the fifth floor of a building in Rue Monge; it was within less than half an hour's walking distance from the hospital.

He used to leave the building, number 67, halfway along the street, and stroll down towards the river Seine. He would first reach the end of Rue des Ecoles, at the end of which stood the Sorbonne university. Beyond that was the tiny Place Maubert with its lovely garden. Then he would move on to Rue Lagrange by the pharmacy, located on the right-hand corner at the junction of Rue Arcole that took him to Pont d'Arcole over the Seine. As soon as he crossed the bridge, to his right soared the vast awesome building of Notre-Dame cathedral, with its lofty towers. Then to the left he found the huge imposing building of Hôtel-Dieu. He would go in through the great main door that looked over the square, in the middle of which was the statue of Charlemagne mounted on a horse.

His walk along this route was a daily joy. He never tired of gazing at the modern buildings flanking the square, constructed at the turn of the century and inspired by the Art Nouveau style, introduced by French artists, sculptors and designers that dominated popular tastes and thoughts.

The front of each building had a marble panel into which was carved the date of its construction and the name and signature of the architect. These buildings were like the works of artists that you see adorning picture galleries. Here were the names of the architects Guimard, Autant and Bigot, and others that Rida had heard of. He looked at the signatures, one by one. It was as if they were competing for the attention and admiration of the spectator by the elegance of their designs, their beauty and flowing decoration carved into the stone in the form of branches and leaves of trees, of plants entwined around the windows, the columns and the doorways.

He was also delighted by the buildings' decorated balconies, with their varied range of hammered bronze, their windows from which hung flowerpots with plants of different colours, and their roofs that were covered with those bluish-grey zinc slates that gave Paris its distinctive appearance.

The places he like to stop at were the many bookshops on both sides of the street and in the narrow passageways between the coffee-houses and restaurants and shops selling flowers and bread. It was as if this Latin Quarter was designed to provide the people of culture who were active there with sustenance for mind, spirit and body.

He used to linger before the wooden stalls that jutted out from the bookshop on to the pavement, enabling people to inspect what they had – literary books, scientific books and art books with fine bindings. The booksellers displayed them with reduced price tags to attract passers-by to buy them, be they teachers or students.

But what really filled him with wonder and satisfaction was when he learned that the specialist course which he had been sent to Paris to complete would be under one of the most distinguished doctors of France, Professor Félix Joseph de Lapersonne, Head of the Department of Ophthalmology at the Hôtel-Dieu Hospital. This famous professor enjoyed huge respect and a great reputation in the world of medical science. Because of this French medical colleges were always trying to recruit him, and to take advantage of his long experience, his great competence and his famous name. He was not long settled as Dean of the College of Medicine in the city of Lille before the College of Medicine in Paris, with the unanimous votes of the Senate, insisted that he come there. Professor de Lapersonne responded to this request and came to Paris in 1901 as Head of the Department of Ophthalmology at the Hôtel-Dieu Hospital, where students followed the final stages in the college with specialisation in different medical departments, as well as practical experience. Professor de Lapersonne did not give up writing and publishing books and articles, which were considered to be the most important scientific contributions to the development of ways of treating and operating on diseases of the eye.

On the first day he was due to come to the hospital, before he reached the main entrance, he slowly approached the magnificent huge grey buildings, overwhelmed with feelings that were a mixture of reverence and pride. Here he was, with just a few steps to take before he entered these portals where he would find himself part of this ancient edifice of scholarship that had been founded centuries earlier and in which were emblazoned the names of the cream of the crop of distinguished doctors, scholars, professors and surgeons. How could he not be proud to be spending two years in the embrace of this rich history, to which his name would be linked?

And before he placed his first steps within the precincts of the Hôtel-Dieu Hospital, he looked upwards and vowed to God that from that day onwards he would strive with every effort he could muster, and that he would work with every fibre of his being to be worthy of this great foundation to which he would belong and that he would fulfil the scientific mission on which he had been sent in the best way possible.

He did not break this vow...

He had been working five weeks at the hospital when it became clear to Professor de Lapersonne that this doctor, coming from the East to train as a specialist with him, was outstanding among all those who were studying with him in his seriousness, his application and his precision, especially when he took part in surgical operations conducted by the Professor. He made use of every minute in the hospital to increase his medical and scientific knowledge.

In the moments between the surgical operations that he attended or conducted on the first floor, which housed the Sainte Marthe section for eye operations, or the examinations in the Sainte Madeleine section on the second floor, he was always eager to go up to the ophthalmology library on the third floor to extract what he could from books, reviews and research studies.

Within a few months the Professor took two important decisions that filled Rida with happiness and pride. They were an expression of the Professor's appreciation of his efficiency and hard work. First he made him his principal assistant in surgical operations and in the daily examinations of patients, especially in unusual medical cases that called for great care in either diagnosis or treatment.

He then proposed to the members of the council of management of the hospital that they entrust his student to give lectures on ophthalmology to newly graduated students of the Paris College of Medicine. They would come to the Hôtel-Dieu Hospital for this specialism. The council of management agreed unanimously. He was given the designation of Moniteur, and was soon giving lectures alongside the many French professors, teachers and doctors in the hospital.

What made Rida more and more proud of this great Professor with whom fate had allied him was that the Professor gradually relaxed the formal relationship of professor and pupil. He showed a tenderness towards him that was more like a deep-rooted paternal love. Whenever time allowed he was concerned about his pupil's circumstances in Paris, his plans for the future when he moved on and how his country would benefit from what he had learned in France and in the hospital.

In addition to what he was learning in the hospital, he was also gaining a lot from his residence in Paris. In the year of his arrival there, 1909, Paris teemed with political, intellectual, literary and artistic activity of every shape and form.

The President of the Republic at that time, Armand Fallières, was the first President in the history of France to take over in a natural manner from his predecessor. All the previous presidencies had ended either in resignation or in death. Then there was no obvious successor who took over from a predecessor. During Fallières' presidency, the property of the French churches and monasteries was confiscated following a decision taken by both the Chamber of Deputies and the

Senate to separate the Church from the State. This historic decision allowed France to liberate itself from the outdated bonds of the past and from submission to religious authority. It found itself truly launched on a road to modernity and contemporaneity.

In the year of Rida's arrival in Paris, Aristide Briand replaced Georges Clemenceau as Prime Minister. And in that year the distinguished mathematician and philosopher Henri Poincaré became a member of the French Academy. A number of Paris Métro lines were completed and a start was made to provide some of the stations with escalators. In this year news of flying mania filled the front pages of the newspapers with articles about aviation attempts. None lasted more than a few minutes, during which a small plane took off and soon afterwards flopped back to land. But when the aviator Blériot succeeded in crossing the English Channel by air in a plane he designed himself, the newspaper *Le Temps* reported, "This is an historic day that will have an everlasting impact in the annals of science and civilisation." In this same year André Gide published his novel *La Porte Etroite*, which critics considered one of the most important of his works. And Paris witnessed the first performances of the Russian Ballet under the direction of Diaghilev. It dazzled the French with a new unfamiliar style it brought with its ballet, both in the manner of dancing, in wardrobe design or the scenery created by the painter Pablo Picasso, and even in the posters about the performances produced by the writer and painter Jean Cocteau. In this year *Le Figaro* published on its front

pages the first manifesto about Futurism in art, written by
Marinetti, which created an enormous stir in intellectual and
artistic circles.

After the train left the station at Homs heading for Riyaq,
rain started to pour down as night fell, covering the land-
scape with a veil of darkness.

Rida wiped away with his hand the condensation on the
window. He could only just make out the trees alongside
the line as they flashed past like spectres dancing in the dark
under the downpour. Images of his life returned to him,
vying with each other and coming to him one after another,
taking him to another rainy autumn day in Paris eight years
earlier.

On that day in 1910 Rida came down from his flat as usual
early in the morning. As he left the main door of the building
he noticed that the sky was somewhat cloudy. He stretched
out his hand, as Parisians are wont to do, to see whether rain
was in the air, and he felt a few drops of light drizzle. "It's
a passing cloud," he said to himself. He walked down the
Rue Monge on his familiar daily route. The light rain turned
heavier. He took no notice and did not think it necessary
to go back to his flat to fetch his umbrella. He had an early
meeting with his professor to discuss the exceptional case of
one of his patients. He quickened his pace.

But as he approached Rue des Écoles there was a sudden

flash of lightning. Then a clap of thunder shook the windows of the buildings. He looked up to the sky and saw it covered with thick black clouds. He had been unaware of these when he was leaving his flat. They were soon above the heart of the city, and it began to rain heavily. Then a sudden violent gust of wind almost tore off the branches of the trees and snatched the umbrellas from the hands of passers-by as they raced to seek shelter in the entrances of the arcades. Soon the streets and pavements disappeared beneath streams of water that had fallen with speed and intensity and were now heading for the Seine.

Although the water had drowned Place Maubert when he got there, he nonetheless crossed it, for he had no alternative but either to wait or to go back. His aim was to get to the hospital. He walked and leapt through the pool of water that had formed in the square, the water coming over his ankles and his clothes dripping with water. He reached Rue Lagrange and paused, panting, leaning against the wall of the pharmacy located on the corner to get his breath back and to shake off some of the water that had drenched his clothes and shoes before he resumed his journey to the hospital. Moments later he heard, as if it was coming through the noise of the pouring rain, a voice that was not clear.

"Monsieur, monsieur."

At first he could not work out where this faint feminine voice was coming from or what it meant. The call was repeated, this time more distinctly. He could not see anyone on the deserted pavement who might be calling to him. He turned towards the door of the pharmacy, which was slightly ajar. Looking out was a dignified white-haired elderly lady. She was actually looking into his pleading eyes.

"Monsieur," she repeated, her voice full of compassion. "Yes, it's you I'm speaking to. I think if you were to shelter here in the pharmacy for a few minutes, the rain won't soak you any more than it has done already."

He responded automatically to this unexpected kind invitation and entered the pharmacy. With embarrassment he muttered a few words, a mixture of thanks and apology for the rainwater that was dripping from his clothes and shoes onto the fine marble floor.

He looked at her with shy fleeting glances.

"Don't worry," she said. "We'll bring you a towel so you can dry your clothes."

He could not realise why she spoke so decisively until she said, "Marcelle, Marcelle, bring a towel, please."

There was a door between two cabinets in which were displayed bottles of medicine, and a young lady of about twenty emerged, bright-faced and wearing no make-up. What enhanced the innocence of her face was that she was wearing the white working overalls worn by doctors, pharmacists and nurses. She came in, bringing a towel.

"This is my granddaughter, Marcelle."

The lady took the towel from her and handed it to Rida. He thanked her and also the granddaughter, who quickly withdrew to the room behind the cabinets which housed the pharmacy's office and laboratory.

"Let your clothes dry out awhile. Why not wait here until the storm passes and the rain stops."

"I don't know how to thank you, madame, for these kind acts. But I must get going at once and continue my way to the Hétel-Dieu Hospital."

"Oh dear, are you unwell, monsieur?"

"No, I'm a doctor."

He said this with a smile, as he continued to dry his clothes.

"I must keep an appointment with my teacher, Professor de Lapersonne."

"Do you mean the head of the Ophthalmology Department at the hospital?"

"Exactly so. I'm following a specialisation under him."

"What a happy coincidence! He's a close friend. He was a colleague of my late son, Jules, and his wife, Henriette, who founded this pharmacy. He calls on us every now and then to make sure that I and their daughter, my grandchild, Marcelle, are all right. He's a man in a million. Please tell the Professor that Madame Eugénie Olbiet sends her greetings."

She then added in a charming manner, "May I know the name of our friend's pupil?"

"My apologies for not having introduced myself. My name is Rida Saïd."

"Your name has an oriental ring."

"Yes, I'm from Damascus."

"Another great encounter, in that this Parisian storm has brought to our pharmacy a doctor from that distant land!

"We are honoured to know you, and, seeing you are in a hurry, let me lend you an umbrella that will keep you dry from the rain on your way to the hospital. Anyway it's just a passing autumn storm. The rain will stop after a while. If you return by here you will be able to drop in and give us back the umbrella. The pharmacy does not close until seven in the evening."

"Yes, this is the way I come back. I live in this quarter, in Rue Monge nearby. Thank you again for everything. I will pass on your greetings to the Professor. We'll meet again."

When Rida reached the entrance hall of the hospital, he met his professor, who looked at his drenched clothes. He smiled and said challengingly, "No one would say that you actually had an umbrella if they saw you in this state."

Rida told him that he only had an umbrella at the end of his way there, and that he had borrowed it from Madame Eugénie Olbiet, who sent him her greetings.

Did he realise that the storm that had forced people walking along Rue Lagrange to take refuge from the wind and the rain in the entrances of buildings had, in his case, driven him not into a block of flats, but to a new phase in his life?

When he leant against the wall of that pharmacy to get his breath back and then responded to the gentle invitation to come and shelter from the storm, it did not occur to him that his quick response was not to the voice of Madame Eugénie, but to a voice whose name was Destiny.

How remarkable is this Destiny! How remarkable it was that that rainy day became the beginning of a new page in the book of his life, linking him with the two women of the pharmacy in a unique genuine warm friendship and affection. He returned the umbrella and, as an expression of his gratitude, invited them to have tea with him on the following evening in the Café Luca Boulard, the wide windows of which overlooked the crossroads of Boulevarde Saint Michel and the Luxembourg Gardens. He realised from the first of many conversations with them that they embraced culture of every kind. He was also surprised that they knew a lot about his country, derived from the books of writers, diarists and travellers who had visited the East. These included Maxime du Camp and Pierre Loti. Marcelle actually knew by heart the poem Lamartine had written in April 1833 describing the houses of Damascus, with their interior courtyards adorned with flowers, trees and fountains, and the way of life in them.

As he discussed with Marcelle Paris's boundless cultural activities and talked about the prevailing new currents and trends, he realised how close they were in their intellectual and artistic tastes, attitudes and opinions. Outside their scientific training, she in pharmacy and he in medicine, they followed closely what was coming up in the Parisian cultural sphere. They would discuss the different schools of artistic thought – the paintings of Picasso, Braque, Léger and Matisse, and the music of Debussy, Fauré, Ravel and Stravinsky. They would talk about the books of Edmond Rostand, Tristan Bernard and the plays of Lucien Guitry.

When they went one weekend to the autumn exhibition at the Grand Palais, they took with them his friend and colleague in medical studies, Ahmad Qadri, in order to take him out of the whirlpool of his frenetic political activity. Ahmad was setting up the management of the society for Young Arabs in Paris, al-Fatat al-Arabiya.[1] It was a most important exhibition where they enjoyed the work of Monet, Pissaro, Renoir, Sisley, Rodin and Maillol. Dr Ahmad Qadri was delighted with this special day, which refreshed him, giving him an insight into an aspect of Parisian cultural life that his political preoccupations had not let him become familiar with. He also expressed his pleasure at meeting this cultured young lady Marcelle. He listened intently to her evaluation of the exhibition at tea in the café near the Grand Palais.

After they took her back to the Métro station from where she went back to her home, Rida strolled with his friend Ahmad down the broad Champs-Élysées towards the Place de la Concorde, enjoying the warm autumn sun before each of them went to their separate homes.

As they were deep in conversation Rida imagined he heard the words, "Have you thought of getting engaged to her?"

It was a question his friend Ahmad dropped quietly and hesitantly. Rida was not sure that he had heard these words. He made no reply and his friend did not repeat the question.

On his way to Rue Monge questions started to turn themselves over in his mind. Did the question come as a surprise? Did something unspoken and hidden in his mind come as a question from his friend to set him off thinking? What was it that made him seek for stronger bonds for this special friendship with Madame Olbiet and her granddaughter? Perhaps he saw in the face of Eugénie the face of the mother he never knew and whose indistinct image had haunted his consciousness since his early childhood? Who knows – this woman might actually be like his mother. And what about Marcelle? Like him she was an orphan; she had lost her parents in a terrible accident, while he had lost his mother. In her refinement and her gentle conversation she resembled the women of his own country. He was confirmed in the rightness of this view when he learned from Professor de Lapersonne that Marcelle and her grandmother were descended from a distinguished family from the department of Oise near Paris.

Before he went to bed, he made up his mind. He sat down and wrote a long letter to his father asking his permission to ask for the hand of Marcelle, whom he had already written about in earlier letters, describing the nature of the friendship that brought him together with her and her grandmother. He reassured his father about how things were and wrote at length on the details of his studies, his residence and his life in Paris. A few weeks later he received a positive reply, but his father made it a condition that this marriage should not distract him from returning to his homeland.

Then events followed one another fast. He first addressed Madame Eugénie, whose face beamed when she heard his request. But she asked him to take his time while she had a word with Marcelle and with Professor de Lapersonne, who, since her parents' deaths, had been de facto guardian to her granddaughter. Marcelle's departure meant that the pharmacy would close, leaving the grandmother alone in Paris. He immediately told her that he would take them both to Syria so she could be at the side of her granddaughter and live in that Orient that she already knew from afar; it was now the time to see it at close quarters.

He was overcome with happiness when Marcelle gave her consent, and when the Professor gave his blessing to this marriage and backed the idea of Madame Eugénie going with the couple to the East.

The wedding took place on 19 January 1911.

The Professor said he would invite them all to attend a performance of the Russian Ballet. Its third season would start shortly at the Théâtre de Châtelet. He said he would get tickets for the production on 16 June, the day following Rida's graduation from the Hôtel-Dieu and so, he said, "we can celebrate two happy events together."

On that evening they saw the ballet *Petrouchka*, a really brilliant production. Stravinsky's music and the magical worlds created by the founder and Director of the Russian Ballet, Diaghilev, transported them to a peak of elation and delight. What added to their pleasure was the fact that seated near them in the audience was Auguste Renoir, the painter of the times, for whose wonderful Impressionist work they all had the greatest admiration.

When the curtain fell at the end of the final act, the audience gave a prolonged standing ovation for the dancers and musicians. Whenever the curtain was raised in response to the applause and then fell again the audience clapped again and cried out enthusiastically. The curtain rose again and the performers answered the applause with broad smiles and graceful curtseys.

The evening was the triumphant climax of his residence in Paris. As Rida left the Théâtre de Châtelet with the others and saw the lights begin to be extinguished, he realised at that moment that the curtain had fallen on two beautiful years of his life.

He then cast his gaze on the days to come.

Those days approached.

They approached to take him at one time to the peak of happiness and joy, and at other times to the depths of sadness and despondency. But the concerns that preoccupied him from time to time were not enough to plunge him into an abyss of despair or to let him escape pain and grief.

In the depths of his soul he was certain that he had an appointment with the multiple destinies waiting for him at the end of the road, and that there was no doubt that he would rise up to the challenge however overcast the skies and however he was assailed by misfortunes.

If it were otherwise what was the point of returning to his homeland?

Was it not he who persuaded his Syrian fellow military doctors that they should go together to Damascus when they were given the choice either to remain in Istanbul or to be transferred to Damascus?

His vision of the sense of belonging and identity had not changed, after his soul had agonised over the vile futile war in the Balkans and his meeting with his teacher Umar Lutfi. The menace of the growing emphasis on Turkishness that was hostile to Arabs in Istanbul was clear to them both. Then the words of his father about *homeland* and *return to the homeland* came back to him. These insistent words stirred his inner feelings like the sound of hammers on bells.

But a return did not just mean changing one land for another or the transfer from a land of exile to the land of his own people. For him the return was a daily activity, a constant behaviour, an adherence to his birthplace regardless of adversity or the sequence of evil and repulsive acts, of which there was so many!

When he and his military medical colleagues returned to work in the central military hospital, he was very happy. This facility provided the best preparation for medical needs, with all the medicines, tools and drugs needed for examinations and surgical operations, especially in the ophthalmology department, which he was appointed to lead. He was delighted, for the hospital, although it was nominally for the military, was of benefit to many civilians, especially the families of the officers and men. It meant that his excellent medical services would reach a large number of people in greatest need.

Within a few months he noticed that some extraordinary matters were happening in an obscure way. He observed that there was a growing demand for medical treatment around the clock. The hospital was overwhelmed with numbers whose needs exceeded the capacity to absorb them. He began to wonder: "Is this to be the case in some future critical situation?"

Soon the whole country became the theatre for unfamiliar activity. Large military units arrived from Anatolia and northern Iraq. Among them were German forces and equipment. At their head were senior German officers who had commands in detachments of the Fourth Turkish Army based in Syria. The arrival of German soldiers coincided with constant propaganda campaigns to persuade people that the Germans were only confronting France, Britain and Russia in order to defend Islam!

He realised that what was happening was a preparation for a war that Germany was hankering to ignite, dragging Turkey along with her.

In the first week of August 1914 it all happened. This war burst out in Europe and the atmosphere of war was reaching Syria without actually taking place on its soil.

There began to be a widespread transfer of officers and civilians, which included Rida. He was transferred from the Military Hospital to head the Medical Board of the Hijaz Railway. When the Head of the Military Hospital, General Ahmad Nadir Bey, handed over the transfer order, he gave Rida to understand that it was because his efficiency and medical and administrative competence was appreciated. He intimated that the body to which he was being transferred was beset with many complex administrative, organisational and medical problems. He had been chosen to take it out of the chaos. The General added that the transfer would mean that he would not be sent to any new war front that Turkey might be engaged in. He then added with a laugh, "One war in the Balkans is enough for you!"

He was pleased with the transfer because it meant that his medical services from that time would extend beyond just the people of the city. He would be finally disengaging from the military after thirty continuous years since his elementary studies in the Rushdiya Military School in Damascus. For the first time he would become a civilian at a time when the reputation of the military was becoming hateful to the general public, for the government was beginning to use force to requisition whatever the army needed – food, livestock, hides, wood and much else – for the anticipated war. When Turkey at last declared war against the Allies on 29 October 1914 he was certain that Syria would be driven to a darker fate, the outcome of which only God knew.

On one of his visits to his father, General Muhammad

Saïd, who was on his deathbed, the old man, who knew about the outbreak of war, muttered in a feeble but angry voice, "Didn't I tell you that they would get us mixed up in a war that had nothing to do with us? May God save us from the evil they have dumped us in!" He continued to repeat these words until he expired, one week after Turkey entered the war. He died with distress in his heart and forebodings for his country and its people.

These forebodings of his father were a kind of reading of the unknown.

With the start of the war Syria took on strategic significance for Turkey, which sought to control the country with an iron grip. Regional command was entrusted to a dreadful man known for his ruthlessness, tyranny and lust for shedding blood. He delighted in terrorising people and hated Arabs. He was the Minister for Naval Affairs and his name was Jamal Pasha.

After he arrived in Damascus on 5 December 1914, he brought a bad odour to Syria that, during the three years of his governorship, underwent one awful disaster after another. These included the compulsory round-up of tens of thousands of men who were sent to distant battlefronts which they had never heard of nor knew where in the world they were, places such as Chanakkale, Romania, Dobruja, the Caucasus and Suez. They set off never to return. Among the disasters was the way Turkish soldiers plundered and confiscated whatever fell into their hands. They cut down trees and hid the necessities of life. There were outbreaks of epidemics of every kind, such as cholera, typhus, and malaria that slaughtered thousands of men, women and children. There were summary executions and the seizure of goods. The execution of the finest of the Arab nationalists in Beirut and Damascus was the ultimate in the tyranny of Jamal Pasha. When famine wiped out a quarter of a million inhabitants, starving people were eating garbage and then dropping dead in the streets and alleyways. Most people sold whatever they owned, even the windows, bricks and roofs of their houses, in exchange for a handful of corn.

In the face of these awful tragedies afflicting the country Rida called on his assistants on the Medical Board of the Hijaz Railway to provide as many Damascenes as they could with all the medicines they had in the Board's stores. The City Council, taking advantage of his administrative experience, chose him to take the lead in dealing with the famine crisis. He at once embarked on cooperating with charitable societies, mosques and churches to offer, as a priority, all that could keep poverty-stricken children alive. He set up popular organisations in the different quarters to clean the streets, to isolate the sick and to distribute medicine. He also established relief centres to distribute corn that helped to save a large number of people of the district of Duma. This was done with the support of his friend Abdul Qadir al-Azm, the head of the local administration, the *qa'immaqam*, who collected the wheat from the distant villages to provide relief for the people of Damascus.

But the dark night of oppression that burdened Syria and its people did not weaken his firm belief that these sombre times would pass. He was certain that dawn would break after he saw its first signs glimmer on the far horizon. Did Jamal Pasha's tyranny not have cracks in the defeats he suffered on the Suez and Palestinian fronts? He was cheered by the arrival of his second son, Rafic, on 15 March 1917. Only a few months after his birth Jamal Pasha was dismissed and recalled to Istanbul, blamed by the government and its German allies for the defeats in the Near East and for stirring up the Arabs against it. Then the advance forces of the Arab Revolt moved north from the Hijaz under the command of Faisal bin al-Husain after a series of victories over the Turkish garrisons and were approaching the outskirts of Damascus, growing in numbers every day, joined by Arab officers and soldiers absconding from the Turkish Army as it retreated before the pursuing Arab forces.

On the morning of Thursday, 3 October 1918, Damascus woke up to see Prince Faisal entering the city as a hero on a white horse in his Bedu dress, his headdress with a bro-caded *iqal*, his head held high, in the centre of a galaxy of Arab horsemen, their gleaming swords drawn. The city greeted them with songs and bunting; Arab flags were raised everywhere. The crowds that filled the streets, squares and balconies called out *La Illah ila Allah* and *Allahu Akbar*, applauding the victorious army, tossing flowers at them and

The medical team sent from Istanbul to the Military Hospital in Damascus. We see Dr Rida Saïd standing behind General Ahmad Nadir Bey, Director of the Hospital, and surrounded by his colleagues: Abdul Qadir Sirri, Tahir al-Jaza'iri, Ahmad Ratib, Satraki Chan. Damascus, June 1913. (From the archives of the Research Centre for Islamic History, Art and Culture, Istanbul.)

The central building of the Military Hospital in Damascus (under construction) to which Dr Rida Saïd and a number of his fellow doctors were transferred from Istanbul, June 1913. (From the archives of the Research Centre for Islamic History, Art and Culture, Istanbul.)

Dr Rida Saïd when he was working as Assistant to the Professor of Ophthalmology, General As'ad Pasha, at the Military Medical School. (Istanbul, 1908)

General As'ad Pasha, Head of the Department of Ophthalmology at the Military Medical School, Istanbul. It was under him that Dr Rida Saïd studied and whose assistant he became after graduation. (Istanbul, 1908)

Dr Rida Saïd carrying out a surgical operation when he was Assistant to the Head of the Department of Ophthalmology and Ophthalmological Surgery, General As'ad Pasha, in the Military Medical School. (Istanbul, 1908)

The building of the Hôtel-Dieu de Paris Hospital, where Dr Rida Saïd specialised in ophthalmology and ophthalmological surgery between 1909 and 1911.

Professor Félix Joseph de Lapersonne, Head of the Department of Ophthalmology at the Hôtel-Dieu Hospital, Paris. (From the archives of the Documentation Library of the Hospitals of Paris.)

Professor Félix Joseph de Lapersonne carrying out a surgical operation in the presence of his assistants and students, among them Dr Rida Saïd, Assistant Professor. (Paris, 1910)

Dr Rida Saïd with a group of students and nurses, men and women, at the Central Military Hospital. (Damascus, 1913)

Dr Rida Saïd among the professors of the Arab Medical School and its graduates, 1920, during the period of the Faisal monarchy. These graduates included the second batch of doctors to graduate during the reign of King Faisal. The doctors to be seen to the left of Dr Rida Saïd: Tahir al-Jaza'iri, Munif al-A'idi, Abdul Rahman al-Qanawati. And to his right: Dr Michel Shamandi and Dr Ahmad Hamdi al-Khayyat, and behind him, Dr Ahmad Ratib.

Dr Rida Saïd on his graduation from the
School of Medicine. (Istanbul, 1902)

Madame Marcelle Holbe (born in Méru, France,
in 1891, and died in Aleppo in 1918), the first wife of
Dr Rida Saïd. They were married on 19 January 1911.

Prince Faisal bin al-Husain on the balcony of the Baron Hotel, Aleppo, reviewing the troops of the Arab Army. He can be seen standing under the flag alongside the Chief of Staff, Yusuf al-Azma, mounted on his white horse. Saturday 9 November 1918. (From the archives of the French Ministry for Foreign Affairs, Paris.) On this day, Dr Rida Saïd met Prince Faisal, who charged him with opening the Arab Medical School in Damascus.

Dr Rida Saïd, flanked on both sides by the professors of the Arab Medical School and the graduates of the 1920–21 term. This was the last term of the Faisal era.

Diploma certificate issued during the Faisal reign by the Medical School in Damascus. This was given to Dr Husni Sabah who was from the first batch of doctors to graduate during the period of the Faisal monarchy in 1919. The certificate is signed by Dr Rida Saïd, Dean of the Medical College, in June 1920. Dr Sabah later became Dean of the Medical College and twice President of the Syrian University.

Dr Rida Saïd when he was elected the first President
of the Syrian University. (1 October 1923)

Dr Rida Saïd, Minister of
Education, and Ata al-Ayubi,
Minister of Justice, in the
Ministry of Subhi Barakat.
(1925)

Dr Rida Saïd among the members of the teaching staff of the Arab Medical
School. In the front row can be seen: Dr Mustafa Shawqi, Dr Tahir al-Jaza'iri,
Dr Michel Shamandi, Dr Sami al-Sati and Dr Murshid Khatir. In the second
row can be seen: Dr Nazmi al-Kabbani, Dr Munif al-A'idi, Dr Abdul Wahhab
al-Qanawati, Dr Shawkat al-Jarrah and Dr Hamdi al-Khayyat. (1924)

Dr Rida Saïd among his guests in the garden of his house, in the Sikka bi'l-Afif/Muhajirin quarter in Damascus. On his right can be seen: Dr Murshid Khatir, Dr Mustafa Shawqi, and two professors of the Arab Medical School. On the far left: Dr Shawkat al-Jarrah, Professor of Organic Chemistry at the School. (1925)

Dr Rida Saïd among the teaching staff and assistants of the Syrian University celebrating his appointment as Minister of Education, Damascus, 1925. To his right can be seen Professors: Shakir al-Hanbali, Dr Lecercle, Tahir al-Jaza'iri, Sami al-Sati, Munif al-A'idi and Mustafa Shawqi; and to his left Professors: Abdul Qadir al-Azm, Abdul Qadir al-Maghrabi, Adib al-Ja'fari, Abdul Qadir Sirri, Abdul Wahhab al-Qanawati and Shawkat al-Jarrah. In the second row can be seen Professors: Nazmi al-Kabbani, Dr Genestet, Shawkat al-Shatti and Michel Khuri.

During the celebration hosted by the President of the University and Minister of Education, Dr Rida Saïd, to celebrate the release of two professors of the Faculty of Law – Faris al-Khuri and Fawzi al-Ghazzi – from their detention on Arwad Island by the French Mandate authorities. (November 1925)

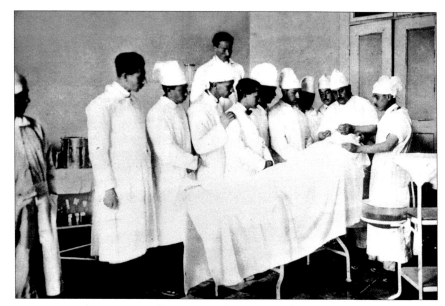

In the presence of trainee students, Dr Rida Saïd conducting
a surgical operation in the Ophthalmological Operating
Theatre at the National Hospital of Damascus. (1922)

Dr Rida Saïd among the staff of the Arab Medical School. Among them
can be seen in military uniform the French doctors assigned to teach in the
School; they are Drs Genestet, Trabaut, Chabot and Soulet. The Syrians, all
doctors, are: in the first row, Adib al-Ja'fari, Michel Shamandi, Rida Saïd, Sami
al-Sati, Murshid Khatir. In the second row, Ahmad Hamdi al-Khayyat, Abdul
Wahhab al-Qanawati, Shawkat al-Jarrah, Husni Sabah, Nazmi al-Kabbani, Atif
Tawakkulna, Michel al-Khuri, Shawkat al-Shatti, Adib al-Habbal. In the third
row, Michel Homsi, Nadir al-Sati, Jamil Kabbara, Abdul Latif Hasaki. (1925)

The President and Dean, Dr Rida Saïd, between the French High Commissioner, Henri de Jouvenel, and Colonel Georges Catroux, during their visit to the Arab Medical School. (2 May 1926)

In the Azm Palace, Prime Minister Damad Ahmad Nami and a number of members of his third ministry. (1927)

At the grand banquet hosted by Dr Rida Saïd at his house in Damascus on behalf of the Syrian University in honour of the theatre companies of George Abyad and Yusuf Wahbi, known as Ramses. (May 1929)

The examination taken by the students of the Law College in the academic year 1928–29, in the meeting room at the auditorium of the Syrian University. Dr Rida Saïd can be seen between two members of the committee for overseeing examinations, Professor Abdul Qadir al-Azm, Dean of the School of Law, and Professor Faris al-Khuri, Professor of Financial Affairs in the School of Law and later Prime Minister.

spraying them with perfume. It was a day unparalleled in the history of Damascus; nothing like it had been seen for centuries. It was a day on which the Arab dream was realised, when a state was established that gave back to the Arabs their bygone glories, restoring once again their civilisation.

But Rida Saïd's celebration of this great occasion did not last long, for the happy atmosphere was clouded when his wife suffered from a heavy fever. He was afraid that she was struck down by the typhoid fever that he and his colleagues were dealing with in different parts of Damascus, along with other calamities. He was working night and day to safeguard the people of the city from the disease. How could it have eluded him and reached the heart of his own household?

In order to check his misgivings he got in touch with a number of his medical friends who were specialists and they rushed to his assistance. They stayed at his side monitoring his wife's condition round the clock. Her temperature rose steadily each day. She then suffered acute headaches, accompanied by general lethargy and terrible giddiness. They tried to bring the temperature down by swathing her with ice. But the fever was obstinate and the temperature continued to rise, until it stabilised at forty degrees. For several days it did not shift from there. When the patient suffered from pains in her stomach and constant nausea, Rida and his colleagues were greatly alarmed as they realised that she was suffering from typhoid fever. His colleagues pointed out the need to get on top of things and, now the war was over and it was possible to travel, to move her as quickly as possible out of the country. It might be that there were new effective medicines that could make her better.

He decided to accompany her himself at once to France with his two sons and her grandmother. He telegraphed a colleague in the Hôtel-Dieu Hospital to tell them he was coming with his sick wife on the Orient Express, travelling from Aleppo via Istanbul to Paris.

He was racing to get her to France before her situation became critical and even worse... but Destiny was faster.

On their arrival at Aleppo station he saw she had symptoms that filled him with alarm. These were internal bleeding, a bad sign in a condition such as hers. He asked the grandmother to go ahead with the two boys to the Baron Hotel where his friend, the hotel proprietor Armin Mazloumian, checked them into two rooms. He then rushed his wife off to the nearest hospital where he hoped to find a doctor on duty who could stop the haemorrhage and save her life. The whole of Aleppo, old and young, had gone out to welcome Prince Faisal who had come to the city with his entourage on a tour of the northern Syrian cities after his arrival in Damascus.

But the efforts the doctor made to save her were in vain. It was God's will to take her from this world early on Friday, 8 November 1918, before they could continue their journey to France. Her resting place is in Aleppo, not in the town of Méru in the French department of Oise where she was born, nor in Damascus, which she loved before she had seen it and where she lived for more than five years, sharing the ups and downs of life with him.

After paying his final respects, hastily and immediately because of the exceptional circumstances in the city, he left the cemetery overcome with pain and weariness. He walked slowly back to the hotel, trying to pull himself together so he could face her grandmother and his son Adnan with the sad news. Madame Eugénie knew that her granddaughter had been in danger and that the chance of recovery was slight. His son Adnan was not yet six years old but his distracted gaze reflected an inner understanding that something serious had happened to his mother. Throughout the journey from Damascus he had been sobbing silently as had the adults. As for Rafic, fate decreed that, like his father, he would only later become aware that he had lost a parent when he was a baby.

When just before sunset Rida was within reach of the Baron Hotel he could hardly see it because of the crowds of people around him. They filled the roads leading to the hotel as well as the entrance, the stairs and wide balcony. They were waving Arab flags and shouting. He found out that Prince Faisal was staying at the hotel.

When he was, with difficulty, able to make his way through the crowd to the hotel and reach the hotel lobby, which was also crowded with officers of the Arab Army and companions of Prince Faisal, his friend Armin waved to him from behind the hotel reception desk and hurried to welcome him. He gave him a hug and took him away from the crowd in the lobby to an inner staircase.

"We have been very worried about you," he said as they

went up the steps. "We have been expecting you back all morning. Madame Eugénie kept asking me when you were returning or whether I had heard anything from you. I haven't been able to leave the hotel for a single minute since Prince Faisal arrived two days ago. Anyway I didn't know where I would find you or to which hospital you went. Tell me, how is your wife now?"

"She has departed for eternity."

"My God! What is it you are saying? What a misfortune! May Allah have mercy on her soul and give you strength. Shall we go straightaway to my office so you can compose yourself before I take you to your room?"

Rida accepted the suggestion and went with him to his office on the second floor. But he sat in silence all the time.

Armin then realised that he had to start the conversation. He told him, in one continuous monologue, his news, the news of what had been happening in Aleppo over the last few critical days, thinking it might distract him.

"If you permit I can tell you in Turkish, because there are many Arab words that I still do know or that I find difficult.

"First of all, you will find that, because I have reserved all the rooms of the hotel for Prince Faisal and his entourage, I have taken the liberty of accommodating you in the section put aside for myself and my family. We left this to stay with some relations, the Khanjians, immediately after the arrival of Mustafa Kemal and the remnants of the Turkish Army in Aleppo twenty days ago. We learned that they had retreated from Riyaq, Ba'lbak, Homs, Hama and Ma'rrat under the pressure of assaults from Arab forces. When they arrived here they took over the responsibility of the city after the German commander, Liman von Sanders, relinquished it. He had been the first to occupy our hotel and make it his command base. He installed machine guns on the roof. A few days ago fighting reached the outskirts of the city. This developed into fierce battles between Arab and Turkish forces that were scattered in our streets. Mustafa Kemal was the target of assassination attempts by hand grenade, and was obliged to retreat just thirteen days ago. He left Aleppo on 26 October.

"While Arab forces were engaging with what was left of the Turkish Army outside Aleppo, chaos spread throughout the city, with acts of looting and pillage. We heard that crowds of people were heading for our hotel, intent on burning and destroying it, seeing it as a symbol of the oppressive Turkish command. We were saved by the influential Aleppo notable, Mar'i Pasha al-Mallah,[2] who was quick in answering our call for help. He came with his men and they were able to disperse the people who wanted to attack us as they arrived in the vicinity of the hotel. It was explained to them that the Baron Hotel would be in the hands of Prince Faisal and his Arab Army. If that had not happened our hotel would have been turned into a pile of rubble. When I heard that you and your family were coming to Aleppo, I took my family to some relations so you could take their place at the hotel."

Armin paused at this point, sensing that Dr Rida was hearing his long narrative but not listening to it with all his attention. He got up.

"Please let me leave you to yourself now," he said. "When you want to retire to your room, it's at the end of the corridor. Here's the key. I believe Madame Eugénie is waiting for you in the room next to it. We have prepared it for her and the children. If you have any need of anything, please don't hesitate to call the reception desk where I will be all night long."

Rida and Eugénie were both up all night, each of them in armchairs by the sleeping infants. Madame Eugénie quietly sobbed but was unable to keep her tears back. He was torn among images of his life, distant and recent, as they unfolded rapidly in his mind. No one image was fixed in in mind's eye before it dissolved to be replaced by another, like flashes of lightning in the sky. He reflected. Could he have imagined this new misfortune that had struck him so unexpectedly? Where was now the confidence in the sunny morrow on that day he had graduated from the Hôtel-Dieu, anticipating future days that he could count as happy, every one of them? There had been no prospect but an unclouded good life.

After the night passed with its long heavy moments, he realised, before he left for his own room, that he had to talk to the grandmother Eugénie about a matter preoccupying him. He said that the blow had fallen and that they had no option but to surrender to the will of Destiny. He wanted to consult her about what he should do now. He reminded her how he had insisted, when he married Marcelle, that she accompany them to the East and not stay by herself in Paris. And now today he was beset with the feeling that he had been responsible for changing the course of her life and for the tragedies she had encountered during the war in Damascus. So he had to ask her, after the passing of her granddaughter, whether she wanted him to continue to go with her to France. There she could make up her mind whether to stay in France, where she came from and had her people, or whether to come back with him and the two children to Damascus.

For some time the grandmother remained silent. When she got her words together she thanked him for giving her this option. She told him in her turn that her fate was linked with theirs, that his family had become her people and that Damascus had become her home. Then she wondered, what about the two children, Adnan and Rafic? Were they not a trust left to her by Marcelle? Was it not her duty therefore to look after them and to watch over their upbringing as long as she was alive? Eugénie expressed her surprise that he took on the responsibility for what had happened to her during the war in Damascus. She asked him, "Have we not heard that France also lived through the misfortunes of war, and had similarly been afflicted by famine, despair and devastation? War is war in whatever land it takes place. If I had stayed in France I would not have been any better off."

She paused to wipe away a tear from her cheek, and then said, "Let's go back to Damascus."

He was half-asleep when the phone in his room rang. He heard Armin's voice, apologising for contacting him at that early hour, but he wanted to tell him that his friend Dr Ahmad Qadri, adviser and personal physician to Prince Faisal, knew he was there in the hotel and had heard about his terrible loss. He would like to call on him as soon as he had finished a meeting with the Prince.

When they met, Dr Ahmad rushed towards him and embraced him warmly, repeating with intense feeling, "*La hawla wa la quwata ila bi-llah*, There is no power and no strength save in God, Rida. There is no power and no strength save in God.

"When I heard the news," he went on, "I was thunder-struck. I was also surprised you were in Aleppo. It was tough that your tragedy and distress has coincided with the happiness of Aleppo with Faisal."

"It is God's will, Ahmad. Thank you for coming and your condolences."

"I didn't want to open our conversation with an issue while you were in this state of anxiety. But there is a pressing matter that requires me to see you at once for it cannot be postponed.

"Since our arrival in Damascus with His Highness Prince Faisal he has been preoccupied, as you know, with sorting out the affairs of the country, the administration, and the ruinous public utilities, the task of setting up a modern independent Arab state in every meaning of the word. It is the Arab dream that we have all been hoping for. Do you remember our discussions in Paris?

"I will not conceal from you that for some days I have
been reviewing with His Highness names of people I know
in whose competence and ability to undertake these noble
tasks I have confidence. You have been in the forefront of
those names presented to His Highness. I have spoken to
him about you and your studies, about the posts you have
filled, and about the scientific and administrative abilities for
which you are renowned. When I asked for you in Damascus
I was informed that you were travelling."

"Thank you for this confidence, which is appreciated. But
I now wish to be frank with you. I have not made up my
mind yet what my next step will be after what has happened.
I have temporarily taken leave from the Medical Board of the
Hijaz Railway because I was travelling, and I am not certain
whether I want to go back to them or to retire to my private
clinic."

"Don't worry! The past is the past. We must now look
to another day, to a better tomorrow that has no link to the
past. So I am asking you, my dear Rida, to prepare yourself
so I can present you to His Highness the Prince. He is the
symbol of this tomorrow to which we aspire. I am keen that
you meet him before he travels to Europe to attend the Peace
Conference in Paris. I will shortly escort you to his wing of
the hotel."

When he entered the reception room with his friend
Ahmad, Prince Faisal was standing in the centre near the
wide window with oriental decoration and velvet curtains.
Rida was struck by his towering presence and awesome

appearance. His fine Arab robes emphasised a dignity that brought out his nobility and majesty. His white smiling face had a touch of ruddiness, and suggested an affable and easy-going nature, and his honey-coloured eyes sparkled with shining intelligence. When he spoke, in an agreeable Hijazi accent, there was blended in his voice the gentleness of the settled Arab and the manliness of the pure Bedu.

"You are most welcome, Dr Rida. I have finally met you. I have learned a lot about you from your friend Dr Ahmad. He is indeed a friend! He has told me about your distressing misfortune. *F'inna li'llah w'inna ilaih raji'un*. We are from God and to Him do we return. I pray to God Almighty that He grant you steadfastness and fill you with the appreciation that we have to surrender to His decree, and that for Him nothing small and nothing big afflicts us except by His decree. How good it would be if you were to look on it as if your lost beloved was one of those we have lost due to the Turkish oppression. This has cost our nation thousands and thousands of our sons who were driven to their deaths in distant war zones, as well as innocent souls who have fallen to devastating famine and disease. It behoves us therefore to make these dark days a spur for us to stand shoulder to shoulder and build up our country out of the desolate wasteland left to us by those oppressors. They left us in a state of unbelievable ignorance and chaos. The intellectual and cultural faculties of the great majority of our people have been stultified; they do not understand the meaning of nationalism or freedom – nor even of independence. We must therefore, after the political and military campaign, have a campaign now, proclaiming the banner of science and the enlightenment of our people. Nations only live with knowledge and organisation."

"Allow me, Your Highness, first of all to thank you, for giving me the honour of meeting you, and the opportunity of listening to your noble words, and your constant support for the spread of knowledge. We have been following this support in all Your Highness's addresses since your triumphant entry into Damascus. They have filled us with joy, pride and belief that this is the way to build up our independent Arab state for which you have called with your august father Sharif Husain, may God support him with all possible strength."

"There is never any doubt in my mind," the Prince said, "that the loyal sons of our nation will stand shoulder to shoulder in order to achieve this noble end, and that they will work to raise the dignity of this Arab nation. I was much influenced during my visit to the city of Hama a few days ago on my way to Aleppo, when I found its good people eager to spread education in their city. On the night I met them, after I spoke about the importance of education for our progress, they made a contribution of four thousand golden liras and will collect another eight thousand as expenses for schools.

"As the Turks have left us in a state of backwardness and ignorance, there is no excuse for us now they have left but to establish seats of learning. We must reopen the colleges and build cultural centres.

"It is our duty to do this at once so that we can prove to the whole world that we are worthy of the independence that we have called for. So I think that, before all else, we must make haste to restore the Medical School in Damascus which the Turks transferred to Beirut. It is one of the most important symbols of a nation's civilisation, even though I have heard voices saying we can manage without reopening it, and instead send those who wish to study medicine outside the country. But I thank God that He has given to us your dear friend Dr Ahmad and Dr Mahmud Hamdi Hamuda, the head of the medical team in our Arab Army, and Dr Abdul Qadir Zahra, the Director of Health. They think that the opening of the Medical School in Damascus is a national task that will have an impact on our social and political life. I accept their sound advice.

"I have given instructions to the governor, General Rida Pasha, and to my brother and deputy, Prince Zaid, and to Ustaz Sati' al-Husri, to do what is necessary. In the light of what is known about your excellent scientific and administrative experience, I am relying on you, Dr Rida, to take this on."

"Your Highness," said Dr Rida, "I don't know how to thank you for the confidence you have bestowed, and I ask God Almighty that I may deserve Your Highness's high opinion."

"How I wish," said the Prince, "that I could be in Damascus to follow the tasks of reopening the Medical School and other institutes, but my obligation is to travel to Europe in a few days' time to attend the Peace Conference. I will have to rely on all my loyal brothers to undertake this majestic mission in the best way during my absence that may stretch to some months."

Here Dr Rida sought the Prince's permission to say some things that were going round in his mind.

"Your Highness, we – my friend Dr Ahmad and I – have taken a lot of your time but I would like you to allow me quickly to make two observations on which I would like Your Highness's opinion.

"The first relates to the name of the Medical School. What I would like to suggest is that we give it a new name – the Arab Medical School or the Arab Medical Institute – thereby giving the institution a purely Arab stamp in this auspicious Arab age, especially as the Arabic language must be the language of instruction. The second matter is that we should not see this institute as a place just for graduating doctors, but as a centre for spreading an awareness of health among the general public. From our experience – that is, of myself and my fellow doctors – during the calamities of the epidemics that afflicted our country, it was clear that we have to fight on two fronts: disease, and ignorance of health issues. But for this ignorance the number of victims of those epidemics would have been much smaller. And so I ask you to give us the necessary powers to spread an awareness of health issues, or the first principles at least, among people, societies, schools and clubs in all cities and villages."

"Your two suggestions are excellent and acceptable. I

will issue the necessary instructions for them to be implemented. I beg from our Lord, may He be glorified, to grant you success. May you receive the blessings of God in all you undertake for the good of the country and its people."

When they left their meeting with the Prince, Dr Ahmad said, "That was an excellent meeting, and I reckon His Highness the Prince was satisfied too. I hope you will now excuse me if I go back to him to sign some documents. I will not be away for more than a quarter of an hour. Please be good enough to wait for me in the lobby."

When Dr Ahmad returned he was very happy.

"I was right in what I felt. His Highness has expressed his satisfaction with you personally, with the measured sense of your words and your excellent suggestions. I understand that he is eager that you get back to Damascus so you can work on the establishment of the Arab Medical School, as you wish to name it. He asked me when you will be leaving Aleppo."

"Mr Armin has told me that the first train for Damascus is the Tuesday evening train, that is, in three days' time. We'll be on that, if God permits."

"Good. I will come on the morning you travel to say farewell. But I would like to suggest that you come to the hotel balcony in two hours' time. The Prince will be there with his entourage to review units of the Arab Army that will pass before him to wish him well before he sets off for Paris. The review will be overseen by the Chief of Staff, General Yusuf al-Azmeh. I hope you can bring along your dear son, Adnan. He will be delighted with the sight of this military review."

When Dr Ahmad came on Tuesday morning to say farewell, he told Dr Rida about the meeting held the previous day in the Arab Club, and about the huge crowd of Aleppines who gathered there to welcome His Highness the Prince and asked him to make a speech. He improvised a comprehensive address in which he stressed the points he and Dr Rida had discussed when they met.

Then he wished his friend bon voyage and good luck in the important tasks with which he was charged.

When he came to the doors of the railway station, and before going through with Madame Eugénie and his two sons, he felt he was about to become hostage to a new destiny – a destiny that would take him back again to Damascus, the homeland.

3

THE GIVING

La seule histoire d'une personne humaine, c'est
l'émergence graduelle de son voeu secret à travers sa vie
publique.

The only story of a human being is the gradual
emergence of his inner commitment in the course of his
public life.

Louis Massignon

Thursday, 14 November 1918

As the train very slowly came into the Hijaz Station,[1] Rida
could see through the window the first streaks of dawn on
the distant horizon, peering through the remnants of the
dark clouds that, along with heavy rain, had been with them
throughout the wearisome journey from Aleppo. It had only
stopped pouring just before the end of their journey.

It seemed as if Damascus was greeting him with a new dawn, heralding serenity, and he wondered whether this new dawn would also herald days that would bring light to his life.

As a carriage conveyed Rida, his sons and their great-grandmother from the station, at speed up to Shura Street on the heights of Muhajirin,[2] he reflected on this new turn of fate that had quickly brought him back to his Damascus house only nine days after he had left it. He had then thought he would be away for months and months.

The tumultuous nature of his reflections continued until the carriage stopped in front of the house he had rented from his friend, the pharmacist Sadiq Shura, five years earlier on his return from Istanbul. Sadiq Shura had been among the first to construct modern houses in that district on the slopes of the mountain.

On his arrival he set about unpacking and getting some rest after the trials of the exhausting journey. Then he heard someone knocking persistently at the front door. He went to open it to see who was calling at that early hour. It was his friend and neighbour Sadiq Shura.

"I do apologise for disturbing you, Dr Rida, when dawn has hardly broken," he said after welcoming him home, "but when I heard the sound of the horses' hooves entering the street and stopping at your house I realised that you were back from your travels. I had to rush to tell you that they've asked me about you more than once, for they were expecting you some time or other."

"You're very welcome, my dear Sadiq, but who are we talking about? Who are *they* who are asking you about me and expecting me back?"

"Those who work in the office of the Governor, General Rida Pasha al-Rikabi. He asked me to tell you, as soon as you were back, that you must come to a meeting at eight this morning to be held in his office. He heard from Dr Ahmad Qadri that you had left Aleppo on the Tuesday train."

"Thank you for your concern. I'll be there at the agreed time, inn sha'Allah. But how nice it would have been if you'd sent someone to tell the driver of my own carriage, Abu Yusuf, that I was back so he could take me to the meeting. He is not expecting my return so soon. I wish he had also been asked to bring with him Umm Bashir who used to help us out with household matters."

"Don't worry, I'll look after all that. If we don't find Abu Yusuf, my own driver and carriage will be at your service all day."

When he entered the room of General Rida Pasha, he saw Dr Mahmud Hamdi Hamuda, head doctor in the Arab Army, and Dr Abdul Qadir al-Zahra, Director of Health. After he was greeted warmly, the Governor said, "We are sorry for having been so impatient in getting you to join us in this meeting, which is to look at the issue of medical education. Since His Highness Prince Faisal entered Damascus at the head of our Arab forces at the beginning of last month, his first concern has been to coordinate efforts to build up the institutions and amenities of the country that have been in ruins. After the Turks we had three issues at the top of our list of priorities, namely, establishing security, organising the administration and modernising education.

"Over the last few weeks we have fixed the framework for security and administration, and we are meeting today to discuss the important matter of education. I mean by this the reopening of the Medical School in Damascus, after the Turks had transferred it, as you know, to Beirut. We therefore thought we should meet with you at once to speed this up. We were very happy when Dr Ahmad Qadri told us that His Highness the Prince had selected you to take charge of the school and to carry out this noble task with all it means in terms of language, culture and medical education. You are also well known for the outstanding administrative experience you have demonstrated in all the posts and tasks that have been entrusted to you, at the Central Military Hospital, when you were Director of the Medical Board of the Hijaz Railway and at the Damascus Municipality in the darkest times of war, when you succeeded in relieving the blight of pestilence that was ravaging the people of our city.

"And now what steps do you suggest should be taken to set up the Arab Medical College[3] which we all want? Calling it the Arab Medical School or College was fitting and part of the package of your proposal to His Highness the Prince when you met him in Aleppo."

"First of all," replied Dr Rida Saïd, "I would like to offer my great thanks to everyone who has honoured me and selected me for this task, above all His Highness the Prince. They have given me the opportunity to take part in laying a brick in the edifice of the modern Arab state for which we are all striving. I would also like to express my uttermost appreciation to those distinguished men of medicine, Dr Hamuda and Dr Zahra, for their support. As you know from His Highness, the idea was to found an Arab Medical School (*madrasa*) in Damascus to take the place of the Turkish Medical School (*mektep*), in spite of the fact that many people were opposed to this grand idea.

"As for what has to be done now, as you know, this school, like any other school, needs a site, equipment, a teaching staff and students."

"Talking about students," General Rida Pasha said, "two days ago a number of students who were in the final year at the Turkish Medical School in Beirut came to me – there were about fifty of them – and said that when the afore-mentioned school closed and their studies were interrupted before they graduated, they were very worried about what would happen to them. They wondered how the question of their graduation would be resolved."

"We could form a special class for them to check on what they know and then fill in the gaps in their knowledge. We can then check on their experience and award them certificates of the Arab Medical School that we will be founding.

"Anyway, this is one of the many questions for which there must be appropriate answers at this transitional stage. May I suggest we form a committee that can work rapidly to find answers to these questions?"

"Excellent suggestion! I propose that Dr al-Zahra chairs this committee and that the members of it are – as well as yourself, Dr Rida – Dr Abdul Rahman al-Shahbandar, Dr Mahmud Hamdi Hamuda and Dr Ahmad Munif al-A'idi, and that other members may be co-opted to the committee if it is thought appropriate.[4]

"But what I'd like you to do is to start working at once, bearing in mind that we have allocated 2,000 golden liras towards setting up the Arab Medical School and a School of Law that we aim to open next September if God permits. I would also like you to know that our good friend, Sati' al-Husri, Director of Education, will offer you any help you need in your work; he is responsible for setting up new educational institutions in these auspicious times."

Wednesday, 16 June 1920

He stopped at the top of the steps of the National Hospital[5] and gazed down at the sight below where he stood: the Salimiya Tekke, with its two slender minarets, its domes and ornate arches amid the green meadows and lofty trees whose tints and shadows were reflected in the waters of the rippling River Barada.

How marvellous was this scene that he enjoyed looking at countless times! But since that morning he was overcome with a feeling that he was seeing it for the first time.

He happened to turn to the right where his family home stood, the home where he had been born and where he grew up before his father sent him to Istanbul to study medicine. Who could have imagined that the days would pass to bring him back as Dean of the Arab Medical School that was next to the slopes of Bustan al-A'jam, the Garden of the Persians, where stood the beautiful house that had been the cradle of his infancy and childhood?

He was roused from his musings, which had taken him far away. He set off walking full of happiness towards the school building behind the hospital.

It was early when he came to work this great day to check how well the preparations were going. He was not exaggerating when he described it as an historic day. On this day the first batch of doctors would graduate from the Arab Medical School. They would be given the name "the special group of 1919/20." The route to this day had been crowded with difficulties!

When Prince Faisal had given him the task of reopening the Turkish Medical School[6] in Damascus with the new name of the Arab Medical School, he faced many obstacles and complications that he was able to overcome with his own efforts and the hard work and strong commitment of his colleagues. The building that had been evacuated and neglected during the war was in a state of ruin, and the laboratories and equipment had been transferred to Beirut where they had been dispersed and lost. It was consequently necessary to renew everything and start from nothing. There were insufficient funds to cover the costs of re-equipping the place. The doctors who formed the first teaching staff[7] were obliged to offer their services without pay for the first year.

The second obstacle that he faced was that this teaching body included a number of teachers who were not proficient in the Arabic language, which, it had been decided, should be the language of medical instruction in the infant school. All previous instruction had been in Turkish. This obliged some of them to withdraw, but others – in spite of their age – were keen to teach and worked energetically to master Arabic. They were helped by the enthusiasm of their colleagues who took part in Arabising the curriculum. They saw that it was a pioneering national step forward that was being launched from Damascus. They constantly recalled the great translation movement in science, medicine and philosophy undertaken by their Arab predecessors in the times of the Arab *nahda*.[8] Although his own studies had been in Turkish and French, Dr Rida Saïd was also proficient in Arabic. He used to say "Medicine was taught in Arabic at the American University of Beirut by four American doctors who mastered our language with this objective in mind, and they also wrote medical books in Arabic[9]. It is better for us – for we are the custodians of the Arabic language – to make it the language of instruction in our school." Some professors with a Turkish cultural background preferred nonetheless to stay and meet the linguistic challenges with enthusiasm, making extraordinary efforts to give their teaching in a pure Arabic language. It reached a point that one of them, Dr Sami al-Sati, used to prepare his lessons in a refined Arabic style, and was not too proud to pass what he had written to one of the language experts for correction. But this expert found that there was no need to correct the text, and no need for him to rewrite it. Dr al-Sati would stay up all night learning his lecture by heart. In the morning he would go and deliver it to the students as he had memorised it in flawless Arabic.

There is no doubt that Sati' al-Husri, Director of Education, had a conspicuous part in silencing those voices opposing the teaching of medicine in Arabic.[10] He used to say that our language is what confirms our national identity. It is what unites the Arab people who are eager for the unity we call for. How can we achieve this unity that we want without using the most important basis for that unity, namely, the Arabic language?

While he was wandering around the hall, looking at the workers as they were getting it ready for the graduation celebration, he met the calligrapher, Mamduh,[11] carrying a bundle of certificates for the graduates. He presented them to Dr Rida and they sat together at a side table and he checked them, one by one, to be sure that the names of the forty-eight graduates[12] were spelt correctly. He then thanked the calligrapher, who said diffidently, "You must excuse me, Dr Rida, if I ask you something relating to my work of writing these names all day. The diploma certificate is headed with the words, 'The Kingdom of Syria', followed by 'The Syrian University' and 'The Medical School'. I know that we are living under the auspices of His Majesty King Faisal, may

God preserve him, and we have a Medical School and a Law School. But I do not know that we have a university yet. Has this term slipped into the certificate by mistake?"

At this point Dr Rida's face lit up with a smile and he patted the calligrapher on the back.

"Don't worry about that, my friend," he said. "There is no mistake, but our belief in what we will do makes us go ahead of events. The Syrian University will come soon, sooner than you imagine. Our Medical School and our School of Law[13] are simply the kernel of the future university that will appear shortly in the realm of reality so long as things go on as well as possible, if God permits."

His last words were more like a prayer that everything would go well, for there was a fear inside him that would not go... a fear for his homeland and for the newborn Arab kingdom that embodied his dreams and the dreams of those intellectuals and thinkers who were close to him. They recognised the merit of this noble Arab, Faisal, who urged his fellow countrymen to race against time to achieve those cherished objectives, independence and unity. Indeed it was a race against France and Britain who were preparing to stifle the independence of the homeland, claiming that the Arabs were not qualified for it. There was therefore no alternative but to hasten the process of building up a modern state to disprove these claims and to thwart their schemes.

Sir Henry McMahon led Sharif Husain to understand that Britain was ready to escort the Arabs, consisting of the people of Syria, Iraq and the Arabian Peninsula, to unity and independence. On the strength of this, Sharif Husain launched the Arab Revolt in June 1916, joining forces with the Allies against the Turks. But it became clear afterwards that the British were deceiving him and had made an agreement with the French just one month before that agreement with Sharif Husain, that is, in May 1916 (the Sykes-Picot Agreement), with the objective of partitioning the Arab lands among them after the war, and placing these lands under their influence.

Then came the San Remo Agreement on 24 April 1920 confirming that partition, stating that Iraq, Palestine and Transjordan would be under British mandates, and that what was left of Syria and Lebanon would be under a French mandate.

The San Remo agreement was a fait accompli which the two states colluded to impose, claiming that it was a response to the actions taken by the Arabs at the Syrian Congress held in Damascus between 1919 and 1920. This Congress had condemned the policies of Britain and France, opposed the policy of mandates and announced the independence of Syria in the three areas – Syria, Lebanon and Palestine. Following that came the declarations of the Congress in subsequent sessions that the country was a constitutional monarchy, that Faisal was the king over all parts of Syria, and allegiance was pledged to him on 8 March 1920.

As confirmation of the unity of Syria, the Congress and the government represented the natural territory of Syria. Because of this they paid scant attention to the Franco-British

RIDA SAÏD

agreements that aimed not only at destroying the idea of
Arab unity, but also at amputating the limbs of Syria itself.

Faisal's many interventions at the Peace Conference in
Versailles in defence of Arab rights bore no fruit and were a
cry in the wilderness. His words reached the ears of the Conference but not their consciences. His later meetings with
the Prime Ministers of Britain, Lloyd George, and of France,
Georges Clemenceau, confirmed for him that Britain was
abandoning its earlier promises and was leaving Syria to the
mercy and ambitions of the French. After he returned from
Europe to Syria for the first time at the end of April 1919
he gave a speech, encouraging people to hold firm to their
principles of freedom and independence. "Independence is
taken, not given," he told them. "We must take it with all the
strength we can muster."

Dr Rida saw that when Faisal spoke about strength he
meant not only military strength, because that alone was not
enough to confront the military might of a Great Power like
France that had emerged victorious from the war, but it also
meant creative strength: creating a homeland and its institutions in contemporary form that confirmed that Syria was
not deficient or backward but had the capability to govern
itself alone without any guardianship or mandate.

Thus the country saw the frenetic start of creating modern
Syria, coordinating efforts to speed up the establishment of
institutions and facilities in different fields – dealing with
the law, the constitution, financial matters, culture, education and security and so on.

The newspaper *al-Asima* ("The Capital") was founded by the Arab government to be its official newspaper. Its Editor-in-Chief was Dr Rida Saïd's friend, Professor Shakir al-Hanbali,[14] whom he had known since they were together in Istanbul. It came out twice a week. The first issues reflected the burning enthusiasm in the breasts of all who were in public service, at all levels, to take part in constructing the cherished modern Arab state.

In this newspaper he found the vehicle he wanted in which to express his ideas and plans for realising these ideas. Since he had reopened the Arab Medical School on 12 January 1919 and been charged with its management, every issue of *al-Asima* had news of the activities of the school or of initiatives he undertook there to raise the standard of medical education and to inform people about medical health.

In the first issue, dated 17 February 1919, for example, the newspaper announced that "he would be giving a lecture on medicine at five every Tuesday afternoon at the school. The lectures are open to anyone." The advantage of this was that it was spreading scientific principles of looking after health among the general public and information about medical science. It published the times of exams at the Medical School and pointed out that any citizen who so wished was able to sit for them. The paper also provided statistics about activities of the National Hospital, the number of examinations and surgical operations carried out there, as well as the issue of patients who were admitted and discharged.

In the issue for 2 August 1919, the paper reported, at his

request, that the National Hospital would treat patients at no charge every morning from the beginning of August and that "this news item should be accompanied by a list of the names of the doctors who would share shifts for treating them". These doctors were Dr Ratib, Dr Shamandi, Dr Sadiq, Dr Sutaraki, Dr Jaza'iri, Dr Ja'fari, Dr Malhas, Dr Khatir, Dr Sami and Dr Saïd. He gave himself more shifts than any of his colleagues. He thus gave a good example in the exercise of this humanitarian duty.

All the time he was concerned with strengthening and obtaining support for the Medical School with finance, equipment and medical staff in any possible way so that it would be equal to the Western medical colleges in which he had studied or about which he had read.

For example, when the group led by the famous Egyptian actor George Abyad came to Damascus to put on some world drama in both Arabic and French in August and September 1919 at the Zahra Dimashq ("Flower of Damascus") Theatre, he made an agreement with George Abyad, then at the peak of his cultural career, that the proceeds of one of the performances should go to the school. In its October 1919 edition, the newspaper published an item about that performance in which the company put on the play *Japanese Honour*.

The response of the great actor was excellent and lasting, for he offered the proceeds not just of that one performance, but whenever he came to Damascus the proceeds of one performance would go to the Medical School. In appreciation for this, Dr Rida Saïd hosted a sumptuous banquet in his honour attended by the top professors of medicine and law.[15]

In its issue of 15 September 1919, the newspaper reported that at the Arab Club a committee had been formed to deal with public health and that Dr Rida Saïd had been elected chairman. The objective of the committee was "to promote an awareness of health issues among the general public."

He was happy with this tireless burst of activity, and his devotion to setting up and supporting institutions and amenities aimed to build up an unassailable nation that would stand steadfast against anyone who had their eyes on it. But this happiness was tempered with anxiety and dismay when news came that on 8 October 1919 General Henri Gouraud was appointed French High Commissioner for Syria and commander of the Army of the Levant. He declared before leaving Paris that he was coming to make the Mandate a reality, disregarding the conclusions reached by the American King-Crane Commission published on 21 August 1919. This had been sent by the American President Woodrow Wilson to the region and had toured Syria between May and June that year to inquire about the wishes of Syrians, who told them that they unequivocally rejected the notion of mandates, especially a French mandate, stating that Syria was quite capable of ruling itself.

From what he had read and heard he already knew that

this military man was an extreme symbol of cruel repression, which he had already practised in Morocco. In addition to his religious bigotry he supported the imperialistic tendencies of the French Colonialist Party. This party's political influence had increased after the fall of Georges Clemenceau in the presidential elections, and the emergence of Alexandre Millerand as head of the French government. Millerand was also known for his imperialist aspirations, which aimed to extend French influence to the eastern Mediterranean.

Of course there had been earlier indications of French intentions. After Arab forces had entered Damascus General al-Rikabi sent General Shukri Pasha al-Ayubi as his representative to Beirut to raise the Arab flag on official buildings as in Damascus. But only a few days later the French Colonel de Piepape, who had been appointed Military Governor for the western region, pulled down the Arab flag and in its place raised the French flag. Shortly afterwards, French forces disembarked at the port of Beirut, with arms at the ready and in full military display, and spread along the coast, starting at Beirut and ending up at Lattakia and Iskenderun. They thus imposed French military control over the whole littoral. In the presence of the High Commissioner, on 1 September 1919, Georges Picot announced in Beirut the decision of France to establish "Greater Lebanon" to include Mount Lebanon, the city of Beirut, the three districts of Sidon, Tyre and Marjayun, the city of Tripoli and the four Syrian districts of Hasbiya, Rashaya, the Biqa' and Ba'lbak.[16] The Syrian Congress met to protest against this decision that aimed at creating a Greater Lebanon, expanding its boundaries at the expense of Syrian lands.

There was a series of indications that reflected the malign intentions of Britain and France. One was that, even after King Faisal ascended the Syrian throne, in their communications they persisted in addressing him as His Highness the Prince, without acknowledging that he was a king!

All these manoeuvres made Dr Rida anxious and alarmed. He saw nothing good in the French General who arrived in Beirut on 18 November 1919, again confirming his determination to impose a mandate.

He prayed to God that He might preserve his country from the evils that were advancing. Dark portents were knocking at the door.

Wednesday, 24 November 1920

Was it only four months that had passed since the day of Maysalun,[17] since when much had happened to him and his homeland? The shock and oppression made it more like an eternity.

It was difficult for Dr Rida Saïd to see the shattering of a beautiful dream, and the collapse of the structure of that Arab kingdom, with its short life of one hundred and forty days during which Syria enjoyed for the first time the taste of freedom and independence.

Prince Faisal, during his two trips to Europe,[18] did everything he could to protect the rights and independence of the

Arabs from plotting imperialist ambitions, but to no avail. He had imagined that the great states would accept the fait accompli after the legitimate representatives at the Syrian Congress proclaimed independence and pledged allegiance to him as King of Syria. But these states made no acknowledgement of this.

General Gouraud reinforced his army on the coast and mobilised his forces on the eastern borders of Lebanon in preparation for an occupation of Syria, thereby implementing the agreement at San Remo. When King Faisal became aware of the impending danger he travelled again to the Peace Conference at Paris. It might be possible to dispel the shadow of disaster threatening his country but Gouraud prevented him travelling via Beirut unless he agreed to a number of conditions, the most important of which were accepting the French Mandate and disbanding the Arab Army. He then informed the King that if he travelled by any route other than by Beirut, France might not welcome him or pay any attention to him.

From 14 November 1919 Gouraud started sending the King one ultimatum after another. Each contained more impossible conditions than its predecessor. The tone of these threatening ultimata hardened day by day. The King consulted with members of his government, most of whom found it was preferable to accept the French demands rather than enter into a war which they would lose terribly to an army bristling with modern weaponry and aircraft; the Syrians had nothing like that. He then sent a telegram to

Gouraud replying to the latter's conditions. But Gouraud then claimed that the telegram was late in reaching him. He issued orders that the army should advance towards Damascus. He was resolved to occupy Syria regardless of the answer of its government.

As soon as the French occupied Damascus following the battle of Maysalun they made laws charging the King for responsibility for what had happened and forcing him to leave Syria as soon as possible, even though he had formed a new ministry of moderates who wanted to reach an understanding with the occupiers in the hope that this would soften the burden of the oppression,[19] but it became clear that the French intended to remove the Faisal regime and give chase to the King whatever the circumstances. His government advised him to leave Syria with the least delay on 28 July 1920. The people of the Hauran gathered round him when he stopped among them on his way to Haifa, but the French threatened to shell them if he did not leave that region within ten hours.

Gouraud was not content with just destroying the kingdom and independence, but after less than four months he was set on shattering what was left of Syria. Having already sliced off four districts he issued a decree ordering the division of what was left of the country into four statelets: Damascus, Aleppo, the country of the Alawites and Jabal Druze. To each he gave a government that answered directly to him.

And so everything Dr Rida Saïd feared about this ruthless French General since his arrival came to pass. He found that his dream, the dream of Arabs and his Syrian associates, shrank and diminished: from aspiring to complete Arab unity, to having to accept the unity of the natural borders of Syria, then to the hope of keeping hold of Syria itself. But it soon ended with the country being divided into statelets under the rule of the Mandate.

Another thing worried and alarmed him. The French decision to abolish Arab rule in Damascus might mean the dissolution of all that that government had set up, those institutions that symbolised Syrian independence, sovereignty and royal rule.

His heart fluttered when he pondered the fate of the Arab Medical School, for he heard that the French had sinister designs on it because, together with the School of Law, it was among the symbols of the Faisal monarchy, and the two were among the most important achievements of his brief life and a rumour was current that they wanted to close them.

He wondered what he would do if these rumours turned out to be true. Would he be a bystander and watch the school – not yet two years old, during which he had nourished it so it had become part of himself – being wiped out at a stroke of that General's pen? Or should he defend it with the courage with which a father would defend his son, guarding him from life-threatening harm? Or would he opt for a quiet life and resign so that he would not see his infant school slaughtered before his eyes? He feared lest Colonel Georges Catroux, Gouraud's Delegate in Syria, might summon him and tell him of the ill-omened decision to order the closure of the two schools.

In order to anticipate events before being overwhelmed by them, he thought he should talk to his friend Professor Yusuf al-Hakim,[20] a Minister in King Faisal's last government, tell him about his fears and seek his advice about what he ought to do, especially as Yusuf al-Hakim had been close to the King and had spent long sessions with him before he had left Syria. The King must have made his views known to him, and how people in positions of authority in the administration should act after the occupation of the country.

When he saw him and asked whether he should resign before the French closed the Medical School according to the rumours, Professor al-Hakim told him the gist of what the King had said to him and to some ministers in their last meetings with him. He had reviewed developments from the time the Arabs joined the Allies against Turkey following the promises – later broken – to the partition of Arab lands by Britain and France, going on to the imposition of the French Mandate on Syria by brute force.

"I have regrets not about losing the throne," the King had said, "but about what will befall beloved Syria. My advice to you and to all in authority is to persist in your work. Our homeland will not end just by some alien occupation. You must be resolute and steadfast, you must defend your institutions and the interests of the country before all else."

"In the light of this advice given by the King, who was a shining light for us," Professor al-Hakim added, "and bearing in mind the responsibility that has been placed on all our shoulders, my advice, Dr Rida, is not to think for a moment of resignation. It is your duty to stay and defend your school, with argument and that sound logic for which you are well known. My advice is that your meeting with Colonel Catroux might have every benefit. If, first of all, he confirms to you face to face that the rumours about closing the Schools of Medicine and of Law are true, God forbid, then the meeting will be an excellent opportunity for you to present your point of view and to defend the survival of the two schools in a calm and composed manner. This Colonel, as you know, is one of the French liberals and is far from being a fanatic and, in spite of his military rank, is open to discussing matters objectively, and nowhere near mindless imperialist tendencies."

In spite of the reassuring and optimistic words of his friend, Rida continued to be gripped by anxiety before his meeting with Catroux. "Is he not, when all is considered," he said to himself, "the representative of Gouraud, the General who has occupied our homeland, scorning its monarch and chasing him relentlessly out of the country? Is he not the Delegate of that General consumed with hatred and arrogance, who, as soon as he came to Damascus, hastened to the tomb of the heroic Salah al-Din al-Ayubi, to give breath to his Crusader hatred, addressing the tomb with the words, 'We are back, Saladin'? The only reply was silence – the silence of the dignity of the grave in the face of idle prattle."

It was the first time he was meeting a foreign officer. What were his thoughts – a French officer belonging to an army occupying his country? During his years of study in Paris he had many French colleagues and friends both in and outside the College of Medicine. All were models of amiability, excellent company, well mannered. Where did this arrogant Gouraud come from? He was doing harm to his own country, France, more than he was harming Syria and Syrians.

But the picture of Gouraud was wiped out as soon as the image of his school, threatened with death, appeared before his eyes. As he made his way to Catroux's office, he summoned up his courage, determined that his defence of the school would be robust and frank, based on matters of principle from which he would not budge. He kept repeating, "He who has not got the better of horrible things, does not get what he wants."

As he was ushered into the Colonel's office and introduced himself, Catroux stood up and came towards him, shook his hand and wished him well in a gentle and courteous manner. He was invited to take a seat facing him.

"I am most grateful to you for coming to see me, Dr Saïd. If I had not had so much work, I would have come to see you. I wanted to call on you and visit your school. I have been here for less than two months and I was at once drowned in a whirlpool of never-ending work."

When he heard these cordial and courteous words of

welcome, many of the misgivings that had raged in his bosom disappeared.

"I have wanted to meet you," Colonel Catroux went on, "as I have been meeting other Syrian intellectuals, because I want to know what you think about a number of subjects that are of interest to us and also to you. I would like to discuss with you today the subject of the Medical School."

At this point Dr Rida's heart shrunk. He feared the worst, expecting that an order to close down the school would come from the Colonel's lips at any moment.

" ...What I want to tell you is that there are two opinions about the two schools – of Medicine and of Law. Some want to keep them on in Damascus; others think it is possible to dispense with them and that it is enough to have the American and the Jesuit Universities in Beirut – not far away. I will not hide from you that my boss, General Gouraud, has asked me officially – in writing – to take the latter view, that is, to close the two schools in Damascus as the distance between Damascus and Beirut is not great. Bear in mind that I have not written back to the General. I want first to hear your opinion in your capacity as Dean of the Medical School."

Here Dr Rida summoned up all his courage, pulled himself together and replied in a quiet voice and with clear decisive words without any attempt to propitiate. He had to talk as equal to equal.

"I would like to thank you, Colonel, sir, for agreeing to listen to my views before you write back to the General and

I will speak clearly so you may be fully informed about all aspects of the matter. The closure of the school, or any other school at your hands, is a simple matter and requires no more from you than a stroke of the pen. But have you considered what that would mean for France and her reputation in the world?

"France is where I pursued my medical studies. I didn't just learn medicine there, but I expanded what I knew about everything. It was the centre for culture and civilisation. When you describe Paris as being the city of light I don't suppose you mean the lights flashing in its streets but the light of science and art, knowledge of all kinds that radiates from it. Because of that the task of France is to open more schools, colleges and universities, not to close them down.

"The Mandate over us that the League of Nations has entrusted to you aims first of all to take us by the hand along the road of progress until we attain full independence. How does this aim go along with the closing of Syrian schools? Aren't these colleges the means towards this progress and to increasing the number of Syrian doctors and lawyers, as well as the number of those aspiring to enrol in the Schools of Medicine and of Law?"

"But they can study in nearby Beirut," answered Colonel Catroux. "What's wrong with that? Do you think Beirut is on some distant continent? Or on another planet? In France you find plenty of people from Lyons going to study in Paris or Marseilles or in some other French city..."

"Allow me, Colonel, to be frank once more, when I tell

you that you can make Beirut close if you want, and can make it a long way away when you choose.

"In the Ottoman times the administrative provinces and districts were interconnected under the umbrella of one state. The Damascene, for example, felt no difference in residence or work whether it was in his own city or in other cities such as Beirut, Kerak, Tripoli, Acre, Nablus or Jerusalem. But since you and the British have divided up what has been left of the Ottoman state, those administrative provinces and districts have been fragmented and you have placed each of these cities in separate states that you have set up. Kerak, which used to belong to the Province of Syria, is now in Transjordan. Four Syrian administrative units, *qada*s, have recently, thanks to an edict of General Gouraud, become part of Greater Lebanon. And Acre and Nablus, after belonging to the Province of Beirut, are now in Palestine."

"I see that you are distressed about the end of the Ottoman state."

"I'm not saying it's a question of distress. As you know, we were on your side fighting against them. But I am unable to believe that France came here in 1920 to close a school of medicine which the Ottomans had opened in Damascus in 1903 in spite of their policy of keeping people in ignorance, a policy they had practised over the course of four hundred years.

"As for what you say about French students going to study in other French cities, they were travelling around within one state. But here, you have placed Damascus and Beirut in two different states. As a result, Beirut is no longer within reach for the majority of our students. Let us suppose that they go to study there. Who can be sure that they will not enter the American University instead of the Jesuit University, which some of my Lebanese friends tell me has been putting great pressure to have the two Damascus schools closed so that Syrian and Arab students can enrol with them?"

"Yes, it is no longer a secret that the Superior of the Jesuit University, Father Chanteur, and his party have been lobbying to this effect. They gathered round General Gouraud and put pressure on him to close your two schools."

"...And so I fear that you are characterising this measure, if you carry it out, as a religious or sectarian, and not a political measure, at a time when, in France, from the beginning of the century, you have separated religion from the state. You know very well what reactions there may be to such a measure among the Muslim community."

"They apply their pressure by claiming that the closing of the two Damascus schools is in the interests of France..."

"France's real interests lie in maintaining the two Schools, not closing them, especially as we – the Dean of the School of Law, Professor Abdul Qadir al-Azm,[21] and myself – are drawing up plans for the future; we aim to seek the assistance of some French professors to raise our teaching standards and to bring our syllabus in line with French syllabi, so that certificates from our schools are immediately acceptable in your universities."

"I am most grateful to you, Dr Saïd, for your coming

and I promise you that I will take a stand on your side to prevent your two schools from closing. I will use your excellent and clear points in the minute I will write to General Gouraud. I am very optimistic that he will accept my recommendations."[22]

Colonel Catroux then stood up, shook Dr Rida farewell and accompanied him to the door of his office.

Saturday, 1 May 1926

Dr Rida Saïd's office manager informed him that the French High Commission had been in touch to say that the High Commissioner, Count Henri de Jouvenel,[23] was coming the following day, Sunday, to visit the Syrian University and that Colonel Georges Catroux would accompany him.

Heavens above! What a gulf there was between this day and that day in November 1920 when he met Catroux for the first time, and had thought that he had been summoned to be told that the Arab Medical School was to be closed.

Who would have imagined that the day would come when this French Colonel, who had extended a helping hand six years earlier ensuring the survival of the college, was now calling on him, now that the Medical School and the School of Law had become cornerstones of the Syrian University? And that he would be accompanied on this visit by the first High Commissioner who had the idea of coming to the university?

There had been so many glorious stages that had passed

in his life since that time! Activity among all attached to the
school, staff and students, had expanded. There had been
a huge influx of new enrolments, taking Arabic as the language of medical instruction. This gave the Medical School
a distinct personality. It attracted students from all over the
Arab world, east and west, confirming in a practical way that
Damascus was its celebrated meeting-place. In one class you
would see a Syrian student, alongside an Egyptian, an Iraqi,
a Lebanese, a Palestinian and a Tunisian. It changed Damascus from being a capital for science into being a capital for
Arabism.

Dr Rida Saïd believed there was no future for the Arab
nation unless its sons studied all the sciences through the
medium of Arabic. The experience of the Medical School
in the previous six years had proved that Arabic was a language capable of absorbing all the new scientific vocabulary
as well as adapting foreign terminology. This was just as the
ancient Arab scientists had done, adapting words to fit in
with the basics of the Arabic language. The school's professors devoted themselves to translating the most important
foreign medical textbooks into a fine and elegant Arabic and
putting them into the hands of students. These professors
demonstrated that the language was quite capable of absorbing modern scientific terminology. Their work was rich and
flexible in their use of Arabic roots, and arabising words.

With this enthusiasm for the modern medical Arabic
language, he saw that the work on it should not be limited
to the Medical School. So he decided to found a monthly

journal that would establish this language firmly and publicise as widely in the Arab world as possible the terminology created by the professors. He gave Dr Murshid Khatir,[24] Professor at the school, the role of Editor-in-Chief. It had the title *Journal of the Arab Medical School*.[25] Publication and distribution started in January 1924. In his role as Dean of the school he wrote the introduction to the first issue, in which he said the journal was serving the Arab language that was the link between ancient and modern Arab medicine. It would also be a platform for Arab doctors to exchange their experiences and observations. They could cooperate with their colleagues in Damascus on coining new scientific terms and reaching a consensus on them. The journal would ultimately be a vehicle for spreading information about health to non-specialist readers in a language that was straightforward and within everyone's grasp.

Every number of the journal contained articles written or translated by the Professors of Medicine in the school, each on his specialism, and reports of medical conferences held in Syria or abroad.

The journal also published regularly a glossary of medical terms that had been agreed by the Language Committee in the school and together with the equivalent foreign terms. It invited other doctors to comment on the Arabic terms the committee proposed. In a wish for the journal to promote the latest medical developments in the West, it asked the famous French surgeon Dr Lecercle, who had been Professor of Surgery at the college from 1924, to provide the journal with a regular summary of his observations of French hospitals after his return from annual leave in France. He also provided information about the latest findings in medical science there. In this way Lecercle introduced new techniques in modern surgery from which his students, his assistants and readers of the journal might benefit.

As well as articles by the professors at the school, the journal published the findings of medical research translated from foreign languages by outstanding students. The best of these was Dr Izzat Muraidan,[26] who, before he graduated, provided the journal with a number of these important studies. After he became a professor he enriched the journal with learned articles, admired for their up-to-date information, their clear medical language and their smooth and beautiful Arabic style, understood by almost everyone.

The journal covered news of the celebrations that inaugurated the university as well as the annual graduation ceremonies, with reports of the speeches delivered on these occasions. It published the names of all the graduates, men and women. It did this to provide a documentary historical record of the school, its staff and students, and its medical and scientific activities. The journal is a portrait of a time that can be described as an age of openness, of renewal and of passionate enthusiasm.

The Arab Medical School, since the decision to let it survive, was the pivot point of Dr Rida's life and all his concerns. He toiled away to support it and to develop its institutions and equipment so it would be among the ranks of world-class faculties of medicine. From the beginning in 1920 he worked to get a decree from the Council of Ministers to link once again the National Hospital with the Medical School instead of it being attached to the Directorate of Health. He made it clear to the Council of Ministers that every school of medicine had to have a hospital linked to it so the student doctors could practise in it; consequently he publicly defended the funding of this hospital. In the session of the Representative Assembly[27] held on 15 December 1923 devoted to looking at the hospital budget he stood up and asked for an increase in its funding. He pointed out that the hospital was obliged every day to turn away patients who had come from outside the city of Damascus for treatment because there were not enough beds. They were obliged to stay overnight in filthy inns, thereby aggravating their medical condition. He said he was deeply distressed to see patients in the hospital without covering, the building crumbling into ruin and X-ray equipment not functioning. This had led him to go to the minister concerned, hand over the keys of the hospital and ask for it to be closed so long as there was insufficient funding to carry out these essentials.

He pointed out that the Principal of the College of Medicine in the French city of Bordeaux had visited the hospital and asked him about the number of beds there. He had answered that there were one hundred and fifty, and his guest expressed surprise. Bordeaux was smaller than Damascus, in area and population, but in its hospital there were one thousand five hundred beds.

The Chairman of the Budget Committee objected to this comparison between Damascus and Bordeaux on the grounds that "there was a great difference in drawing parallels between France and Syria."

"It is not a question of drawing parallels with figures so much as drawing parallels between the health conditions here and over there," Dr Rida replied. "The health situation with us demands that we have a greater number of beds in the hospital than those in the Bordeaux hospital where the people's needs for treatment are much fewer than the demands of the people of Damascus.

"Allow me, Mr Chairman, to draw your attention to the fact that we do not mean to copy French hospitals, but all we aspire to is to bring our hospitals in line with the practice of the hospitals of the era of the Arab-Islamic renaissance, such as the al-Nuri Bimaristan here in Damascus, which used to have more beds than patients. There is no harm in pointing out that in the Middle Ages there were hospitals like the famous Hôtel-Dieu that used to put three patients in one bed, regardless of what they were suffering from! I don't suppose you want us to do that; but I do ask you to help us in following in the path of our Arab forebears in the age of the scientific renaissance rather than like the French ancestors in their Dark Ages."

It is worth mentioning that the points he made led the Budget Committee to accept his point of view and to agree unanimously to the funding requested.

He worked on making the Medical School and its hospital

impregnable against all that could be taken from them or in the face of lies about them.

Two events made him concerned about the reputation of these two institutions. The first took place in 1921 when he went through a very difficult time following a remark published by the Directorate of Health in the local press. He saw in it an assault on the competence of the laboratories of the Medical School in conducting chemical analyses. His sharp reply in *al-Asima* showed how angry he was at the misrepresentation of the school. The Directorate of Health withdrew what had been said.[28]

The other event happened when the Medical School invited tenders for supplying food to the patients of the National Hospital. The bids were opened and the decision to award the concession was based on price and the quality and nutritional value of the food offered. One day later another bidder whose bid had not been successful came to see Dr Rida Saïd. This man owned one of the local newspapers. He was known for his lack of restraint in his language and for harassing people to get them to do what he wanted. He protested angrily to Dr Rida Saïd about his bid not being accepted, even though it was cheaper than all the others. Dr Rida replied firmly and calmly, "My dear brother, we in the hospital want to offer the patients good food, not the garbage you'd serve up to us." He ended the meeting ignoring the man's raging threats that people had been accustomed to hear from him.

⁓⁊

His commitments to the school and the hospital were piled onto his other commitments to healthcare and raising public awareness of health issues. He was quick to take part in the early stages of a vital project initiated by his friend Professor Lutfi al-Haffar.[29] This was to bring the fresh waters of Ain al-Fijja to the houses of Damascus, ending people's dependence on the waters of the polluted rivers. The project would spare residents from diseases, such as dysentery, cholera and typhoid fever, that killed them in large numbers, in particular those who drank waters from old channels (*tawali'* or *maqasim*) that distributed the water in the quarters of the old city.

He soon replaced Shukri al-Quwwatli,[30] whose extensive political activities obliged him to be frequently away from Damascus, on the board of the private water company.

From the beginning the founders were determined that the project would be a national enterprise, owned by the people of Damascus and having nothing to do with foreign investment. Two other French companies tried to take over and fund the project, by levying a consumption charge that would have been excessive for the general public. The owners of these companies did everything they could to frustrate the Ain al-Fijja project by using their influence with the French Mandate authorities. Indeed on one occasion they resorted to bribing those setting up the project with massive payments to persuade them to withdraw. But the disdain of

Professor Haffar and his colleagues for these wiles led those foreigners to try to undermine the project with ridicule. The French companies spread the rumour that it was an illusory project impossible to realise and did not have proper local financial backing. They said, sarcastically, "They're not going to pay 150,000 golden liras for clear water when they can drink from the Barada for nothing."

But the board did not give in to any of these pressures. In 1923 it managed to get the concession for the project, endorsed with the signature of the French High Commissioner of the time, General Maxime Weygand.[31] The Board had then to work with speed to persuade property owners in Damascus to subscribe in advance, purchasing cubic metres of water that would be open for sale at the price of 30 golden liras per cubic metre. This was to generate the necessary capital to start work. The board in its first discussions looked for the best means of promoting the project, emphasising its national significance and its numerous advantages to win people over to fund it.

From the first sessions of the board Dr Rida offered practical solutions to problems. The members of the board under its Chairman, Professor al-Haffar, would accept his solutions or ask him to take up delicate tasks with national or French authorities, in order to minimise the difficulties that the board faced.

The first of these practical solutions he offered, aiming at reaching more people and persuading them to subscribe, was his suggestion that the city of Damascus be divided into eight areas, in each one of which the task of promoting the project would be allocated to board members who lived in that area. The board accepted this practical suggestion unanimously, and its members went off at once to hold meetings at their homes with notables of the quarters to explain to them the benefits the project would bring them and to their families and to the city in general. They acted quickly to persuade other neighbours to do the same.

He put forward another suggestion that was aimed at extending the range of subscribers by getting the board to meet the Mufti of Damascus and requesting him to ask the preachers at mosques and religious schools to invite people to be subscribers. He reminded them of verses of the Glorious Qur'an that repeatedly mentioned water as "pure" and "blessed" and "unpolluted." God the Almighty had bestowed this boon upon mankind and made it as something that was "a delight for those who drink it."

In like manner the board gave Dr Rida the task of meeting the Delegate of the High Commissioner to ask him to issue an order requiring hotels, restaurants, factories for making food and drinks, hospitals, schools and bakeries to subscribe to the Ain al-Fijja project and use only the project's water. This would prevent the spread of disease and infectious epidemics. The Delegate very soon issued the order required.

One day the board was taken aback by a newspaper article, about which it had no prior knowledge, issuing from the office of the Governor of the State of Damascus, at that time Haqqi al-Azm. It claimed that the final date for subscribing to the project had been extended. The board had told people that an earlier date was final and that there would be no extension. This had been to encourage subscribers to commit themselves without delay. The publication of this item of news emanating from the Governor's office suggested that the board had no say in the matter.

The board held an emergency meeting and decided to send Dr Rida along with the Chairman, Professor al-Haffar, to meet the Governor urgently to brief him of its concerns about this news item. It damaged its credibility in the eyes of the public, and made those wanting to subscribe hesitate and postpone their contribution.

After a lengthy discussion with the Governor, the latter agreed to withdraw the published news item and promised that in future no item would be published that came either from his office or from him personally about the al-Fijja project without reference to and consultation with the board.

The most delicate task which the committee gave Dr Rida was to send him to Beirut to meet the French Secretary General, Monsieur Titrou, requesting him to exempt the project from the payment of customs duties on necessary items such as water pipes and digging implements. The authorities agreed and issued an order to the customs office as required, and all duties were exempt.

The choice always fell on Dr Rida whenever there was a job requiring a gentle style and rational argument. He was well known for these qualities and it led to the granting of his requests in the best way possible.[32]

⟡

Whenever he recalled another stage in his public life of the six preceding years, he would quote the ancient poet,

How much more they were for us, and how less!

Those years were few in number, but rich and varied in events and destiny! During these years he was entrusted with the founding of the Syrian University, after the publication of Order number 132 of 15 June 1923, establishing it.[33] Then came his appointment as its Principal and Chairman of its Council,[34] in addition to his post as Dean of the Medical School.

During these years he extended the university by adding to the School of Medicine and Pharmacy, a School for Dentistry, and two sections for midwives and for nurses. An X-ray laboratory was completed. In subsequent years he saw the Department of Dentistry and the laboratories for Natural History and Chemistry transferred to the nearby Salimiya Tekke. That transfer made it gradually possible to clear hospital rooms used for different administrative functions so that a greater number of beds for patients could take their place. In the tekke he established a major university library with the latest medical and legal publications.

During this period, on one of his academic missions to France, he selected three French professors to teach at the school. They were Dr Lecercle, a surgeon, Dr Jude, a neurologist, and Dr Trabaut, an internal surgeon. He also recruited a French specialist, a dental technician, called Monsieur Genestet.

From the first day of taking up the office of Principal of the University, he decided that there should be a proud, suitable new building. It would include the university administration, a museum and an extensive auditorium for conferences, celebrations and public events. He drew up a robust plan to provide the necessary funds to cover the expenses of the proposed building.

His policy, from beginning to end, was to put the Syrian University on a par with any major Western university and for its qualifications to be acceptable anywhere in the world. When he appointed those French professors, it was not just to make the university syllabus closer to the syllabi of French universities. Each year he invited a panel of French professors to come to Damascus to conduct a comprehensive examinations (a "colloquium," he called it). Before their graduation and in the presence of the panel, students took a theoretical and practical examination in everything they had learnt during their five years at the school. This practice gave Western and especially French universities no option but to accept graduates of the school who went on to complete higher studies and specialisations with them.

He devoted himself to his work and he was proud of all he could imaginably do for the sake of the university. He had the highest standards, and sacrificed himself in the university's service. All this was at the cost of his health and of the time he could snatch to deal with the patients at his private clinic. He faced up to innumerable difficulties and obstacles. He was as solid as a rock until he had overcome every difficulty.

He was hard-working, serious, active, persevering and tireless. He wanted to set an example to his colleagues and students. He worked in the winter in ice and rain, and in the summer under the scorching rays of the sun. He set out from his home in the morning, passed by the faculties and departments of the university and toured the laboratories, the hospital and the clinics, inspecting them and overseeing what was going on. He would give his views and instructions if he saw something that called for comment or guidance. He would then go on to the different administrative departments, the patients' rooms, the classrooms, the workshops for construction and maintenance before reaching the university's headquarters, where he would devote himself to studying projects and proposals that had been submitted to him. He would have meetings concerned with teaching management and sort out their problems. And what a lot of these there were! In the end he would give classes and carry out surgical operations in the Ophthalmology Department.

With this tireless energy he would be constantly at work. He left at three in the afternoon to take two hours' rest, returning to finish off the work that was left over from the morning. He often stayed at the university until a late hour, not leaving before midnight.[35]

One day he added to his programme of touring the university a visit to the School of Law at a time when the Dean, Professor Abdul Qadir al-Azm, was off sick. He wanted to inspect one of the classes. He asked the Professor of Islamic Jurisprudence, Sheikh Sa'id Murad, permission to enter. The

Sheikh was expounding one of the comprehensive articles of the principles from *Majalla al-Ahkam al-Adliya* ("Legal Judgments"), the text of which was, "The ancient is left to its antiquity." After Professor Murad finished his exposition of this article, Dr Rida again asked leave to add a comment to the exposition that he had heard. "This article, my sons," he said, "we must understand, as it is a fundamental principle that anyone who has justice at his disposal must adhere to justice. Evidence must be taken from the legal party even though he is in the right. But this legal principle, which means letting justice stay in the hands of the one who is right, even though there is proof to the contrary, does not allow us to rely on it as a scientific, political or civilisational principle, because that means we are committing ourselves to ancient styles and ways rather than turning away from them, in an age of development, progress and striving for better things; this must be our guiding light and the objective which we have to achieve. For example, we cannot proceed on the path of life at the speed of a camel, while today we live in the age of aeroplanes making it necessary for us to race against time at the speed of aeroplanes."

Here Professor Sa'id Murad commented on his explanations.

"I am grateful to our excellent Principal, Dr Rida Saïd, for having drawn our attention to the necessity of going along with the world and the pursuit of progress, because indeed we have to follow the example of our forebears who gifted a splendid civilisation to human society. This is acknowledged by fair-minded scholars from Europe as having been the foundation of their own civilisation and development. It is therefore our task to muster our intellectual resources and get rid of the ignorance, poverty, weakness and backwardness that is destroying our nation. We can only achieve that goal if we are well educated and hard-working. Our Syrian University promotes this under our admirable Principal, with his enlightened ideas and inexhaustible commitment."

He used to carry out his many important tasks without any regard to the political upheavals and administrative and governmental changes that were following one another in Syria. From the division of the country into statelets, then the experiment of uniting these statelets, to the widespread revolts throughout the country demanding complete independence, to the continuous changing of the French High Commissioners – from Gouraud to Weygand to Sarrail to de Jouvenel... In the face of these political upheavals, his one concern, above all else, was they would not affect the fate of the university or damage its continued progress. He believed deep down that these vicissitudes were insignificant and would vanish like a fleeting mirage. At the end of the day what would be left on the earth would be solid institutions, among which would be this Syrian University because it was built to last, as was the homeland.

Dr Rida used to tell a story about Professor Faris al-Khuri[36] and General Gouraud. Faris al-Khuri and his fellow members of the government were summoned to the General's Palace in al-Muhajirin. Gouraud said dismissively and mockingly,

"Wasn't this palace where Prince Faisal used to live?" Faris al-Khuri replied, "Yes, Your Excellency, this Palace was the residence of the Ottoman Governor, Nazim Pasha, who built it, then came Jamal Pasha and then General Allenby, then King Faisal, and now you yourself are occupying it. All those I've mentioned have moved on, but the palace is still here and we are still here!" Gouraud was lost for words at this cutting comment and made no reply.

At the insistence of his friend Ata al-Ayubi,[37] he agreed to be Minister of Education during the time of the Prime Ministership of Subhi Barakat at the end of General Weygand's time as High Commissioner. He received this post not to become a politician but because he wanted to carry out reforms in secondary education. During his short spell as Minister of Education he was able to set up the foundations of the Syrian baccalaureate.[38]

Deep down Dr Saïd knew that everywhere evil-doers outnumbered people of good will. He also knew that among the French of the Mandate there were evil-doers with sick minds who were inflicting damage on Syria. He opposed with a sense of duty that was no different, in the final analysis, from the efforts of his nationalist contemporaries who came to blows with those evil-doers in their political work or bore arms against them. In this respect, he made a point of hosting a party in honour of two professors in the School of Law, Fawzi al-Ghazzi and Faris al-Khuri, after their release by the French authorities, who had detained them for nationalist activity against the Mandate. In his view, holding the party for the two men on the university premises made it a nationalist demonstration held on the university premises under the eyes and ears of the Mandate authorities.

When he was appointed Minister of Education, the first thing he did was to go into the room of the adviser, who was one of the evil-doers of the French Mandate. He found a pile of countless files on his desk – correspondence and activities on which, without any justification, no action had been taken. Dr Rida told him that he wanted to occupy this room and that the adviser was to be transferred to the room assigned to the Minister. The adviser realised that he had to obey the order of the new Minister and busied himself taking up the files. Dr Rida asked him to leave them where they were as they dealt with work of the Ministry and it was not for the adviser to move them around wherever he went. He then told him firmly he would ask for his advice on any matter whenever he wanted it. He then summoned all the senior staff of the Ministry and asked them to send to him personally all papers and documents and not to seek advice from anyone but himself. The French adviser soon realised he was being cold-shouldered. He was annoyed at being excluded from activities of the Ministry that he used to deal with just as he liked. He resigned and was replaced by another adviser, a much better man, a French Liberal. He was able to approach the Minister with useful advice and to work with him, implementing all he wanted to do, spreading knowledge throughout Syria and achieving progress for the nation and a better life for its sons.

❧

His friend Ata al-Ayubi also had a hand in two matters affecting Dr Rida Saïd's private life.

On holidays and whenever their work allowed them to take a break they both took pleasure in strolling between Ata al-Ayubi's house in al-Afif Street and Dr Rida Saïd's in Shuri Street, walking up and down, talking about life and its sorrows. They would enjoy the pure fresh air with the beautiful views over the green gardens that cascaded down from the mountain heights to the outskirts of the city, meeting the green area of the Ghouta.[39] The gardens of the two Ghoutas, to the west and to the east, were linked together resembling a colourful girdle that embraced the city. From afar the city was like a glittering white gem, surrounded by silk-like emerald stones.

When time permitted they used to go into the nearby orchards, accompanied by Ata al-Ayubi's two sons, Khalid and Ali, and by Dr Rida Saïd's two sons, Adnan and Rafic, who were all of a similar age. They would enjoy themselves, running and jumping about in the shade of the leafy thickly branched trees. Or they would go and pick mulberries and other fruit that clustered on the bushes on the banks of the Bani Yas[40] River, close at hand.

These orchards were, in truth, a paradise providing abundant shade and excellent low-hanging fruit in abundance: figs that were sweet and tasty, walnuts, apricots, almonds, plums and myrtle bushes, as well as berries of various kinds and colours.

During those strolls Dr Rida always stopped in front of the iron gateway of a fine house that was halfway along the busy road, at the sharp bend crossed by the electric tramway as it ascended towards the terminus at the end of Muhajirin. As the tram rounded what seemed a right-angle it caused a sharp screech on the tram line, and this point became known as Hayy al-Sikka, the Line Quarter.

He used to linger and gaze through the metal bars of the gateway of this two-storey house with its roof of red tiles and extensive garden amply adorned with trees, vine trellises and flower-beds planted with roses. Through it all flowed the river Yazid,[41] with its clean babbling waters, which added an extra charm to the place's beauty.

His friend, Ata al-Ayubi, knew the reason for the long pause outside this house. It was like Dr Rida's family home in Bustan al-A'jam, the Persian Garden, the house with its luxuriant garden where he was brought up, as child and young man. He and his brothers, Salih and Munir, had sold it after the death of their father, General Muhammad Saïd, and after building developments required that it be demolished anyway, together with other houses and gardens in the area. He wanted to acquire a house in Hayy al-Sikka in order to relive his past years and to offer his sons, Adnan and Rafic, the chance to enjoy their childhood in a little paradise just as he had enjoyed his childhood in the family home. He also thought he should have a house like this now that he had become Principal of the Syrian University; in contrast to his poky flat in Shura Street it was suitable for his social obligations. He had to receive friends and colleagues – academics, Syrian, Arab and foreign – in a house that had to be extensive and appropriate.

He learnt that the owner of the house was a Turk who had disappeared from the quarter many years earlier. The problem was that nobody knew anything about his present whereabouts. The house remained empty and uninhabited. It was looked after from time to time in a casual way by a man known as Abu Rasmi. He was sent for and quizzed about the absent Turk. But all they got from him was muddled replies that did nothing to quench their thirst for more information.

Ata al-Ayubi concealed information from Dr Rida about the house and its owner, Hashim Bey, who has been known to him. He had been in charge of the administration of education in Damascus at the end of Ottoman times. He had left Syria with the other Turks at the end of the war, and that Abu Rasmi al-Sirawan was his agent. He told Ata al-Ayubi that Hashim Bey did not intend to sell the house when he left Damascus; after that he had heard nothing from him. Ata al-Ayubi found out from friends in Istanbul where Hashim Bey lived and they, without Dr Rida knowing, bombarded Hashim Bey with letters in which they urged him to sell the house, because if it continued to be uninhabited in the years to come it would fall into ruin and collapse.

Ata al-Ayubi, in actual fact, was wanting to prepare a pleasant surprise for his friend, but Hashim Bey was unwilling to

After the celebration marking the opening of the new university building, which included the grand auditorium and the administrative centres of both the Syrian University and the School of Law. This was under the auspices of the Prime Minister, Sheikh Taj al-Din al-Husaini. (10 July 1929)

An aerial view of the auditorium of the Syrian University.

The Law School of the Syrian University. (1927)

The tekke of Sultan Selim in Damascus in which the laboratory and bookshop of the School of Medicine were established before their transfer to the buildings of the school. (1928)

The Chemistry Laboratory in the tekke of Sultan Selim. In the middle can be seen the pharmacist Dr Abdul Wahhab al-Qanawati, who was Professor of Chemistry.

Dr Rida Saïd among the staff and graduates of the Medical School, 1930. Among them is the first Syrian woman to graduate from there, Dr Loris Mahir, who is wearing a hat in the back row. Third to her left is Dr Izzat Muraidan, who later became Dean of the Arab Medical School. In the front row can be seen the Professors: Munif al-A'idi, Michel Shamandi, Lecercle, Abdul Qadir al-Azm, Rida Saïd, Tahir al-Jaza'iri, Sami al-Sati, Mustafa Shawqi and Abdul Qadir Sirri. The professors in the middle row are Nazmi al-Kabbani, Shawkat al-Shatti, Husni Sabah, Ali Rida al-Jundi, Rashid al-Sati and Abdul Wahhab al-Qanawati.

During the eighth Medical Conference held by the Egyptian Medical Society in Damascus in June 1935. The famous Egyptian doctor, President of the Society and chairman of the conference, Dr Ali Pasha Ibrahim, is seated between the Principal of the Syrian University, Dr Rida Saïd, and Dr Munif al-A'idi, Dean of the Syrian Medical School.

Dr Rida Saïd wearing the decorations, Arab and foreign, that he had been awarded in appreciation of his services. These were: Ottoman Medal for Merit, the Majidi Medal, the Medal for the Ottoman War, the Austrian Iron Crown, the ranks of Knight and Officer of the French Légion d'Honneur, the Egyptian Medal for Education, the Medal of the Red Cross and the Syrian Medal for Merit of an Outstanding Achievement.

Madame Kherié Mamiche, the wife of Dr Rida Saïd,
who was the best aid to the endeavours of her husband
in the educational, health and social fields.

Dr Rida and Madame Saïd with Adnan, Rafic and Omayma Saïd. (1934)

The courtyard of the Carmelite High School in Lattakia where the wife of Dr Rida Saïd, Kherié Mamiche, studied and where she learnt French.

Madame Kherié Saïd, third from the right on the platform, with her colleagues who were active in The Drop of Milk Society during their celebration of Mother's Day, with a number of mothers with their infants. (1962)

During the inspection undertaken by the Egyptian women's leader, Madame Huda Sha'rawi, of the Syrian parliament building after it had been exposed to French aggression. In it can be seen members of the Syrian Red Crescent: Madame Kherié Saïd, Madame Adila Baihum al-Jaza'iri and Miss Amal al-Jaza'iri. (8 July 1945)

During the Arab Women's Conference in Cairo in which Madame Kherié Saïd participated as head of the Syrian women's delegation. (1936)

الدّكتور رضا سعيد

مؤسّس الجامعة ورئيسها من سنة ١٣٤١هـ ١٩٢٣م - سنة ١٣٥٤هـ ١٩٣٦م

خرّيجو الجامعة وطلّابها يقرّون بفضله

The commemorative plaque placed by graduates and students of the Syrian
University in recognition of Dr Rida Saïd when he retired in 1936.

Dr Adnan and Sihab Saïd

Rafic and Nemat Saïd

Omayma and
Zouheir Mourabet

Houzama and
Marwan Kabbani

Racha and Munzer Mudarres

Wafic and Rosemary Saïd

The descendants of Dr Rida Saïd visiting the refurbishment of the Al Madraj university building in Damascus, Syria. The building was first constructed under his tenure in 1926 and the refurbishment was completed in 2011.

The majority of the Saïd family gathered in London on the
tenth anniversary of the death of Madame Saïd in 2008.

put the house up for sale. He understood that the Turkish owner still dreamed of returning one day to Damascus and living in his lovely house once more.

But the years went by, one after the other, and with it the fading of Hashim Bey's dream of coming back. Eventually the dream disappeared altogether and he let Abu Rasmi know that he should sell the house.

This meant that his friend's dream to acquire the house would in the end be realised.

The house was transferred to Dr Rida Saïd on Thursday, 15 May 1924.

Ata al-Ayubi had a hand in another of the most important dates in the life of Dr Rida Saïd, 17 July 1925.

One day in September 1924 Ata al-Ayubi told him that that evening he would be calling on a family that had recently come from Beirut to settle opposite his own house in Hayy al-Sikka. The family consisted of a couple and their young daughter, Amal. He was the distinguished judge Prince Mukhtar al-Jaza'iri and he was related to his own wife, Madame Hafiza al-Ayubi. The husband, his wife Madame Adila[42] and Madame Hafiza were all descended from the great warrior Prince Abdul Qadir al-Jaza'iri, who had fought for Algeria and come to Damascus in 1857, making it a home for himself and his followers. Ata al-Ayubi said that the couple would be very happy if he joined him on a visit to them. They had heard a lot about Dr Rida and they would be honoured to get to know him.

That visit was the first of weekly visits exchanged between the three families. The bonds of friendship were strengthened. They would retire to one of the corners of the house where they were meeting, and become immersed in conversation about their activities and exchange views about general matters. Each of them spoke about the ups and downs of their work: Dr Rida in the university, Ata al-Ayubi in politics and Prince Mukhtar al-Jaza'iri in the law.

The ladies, Adila and Hafiza, would sit in the next room, talking about social matters. Madame Adila told her relative about the projects she was burning to set up, dealing with national educational questions, and charitable, social and health societies that would be involved with the emancipation of the women of Syria.

From time to time they talked in whispers about Dr Rida. They both – as Dr Rida heard from Ata al-Ayubi later – reflected on his domestic situation: the huge burden of work with the university and the Medical School, the obligations that required him to make his home available at all hours for large social gatherings. He also had the responsibility of bringing up his two sons, Adnan who was now eleven, and Rafic who was seven, especially after the death of their great-grandmother. She had taken charge of their education and welfare, as well as some of the housekeeping responsibilities, with the help of some female members of the Saïd family who would come from time to time to offer reassurance and assistance. But his present situation made the two ladies concerned for him. They could see that there was a yawning hole in his life and in his house that could only be filled with a wife of a special kind... a lady capable of sharing his vast social responsibilities, a lady with intellectual abilities that were appropriate to his high position and remarkable scholarly standing. She should be well brought up and with a good education, agreeable in company and a good manager so that she could share the daily domestic load and let him concentrate on his work. They both pressed their husbands to persuade Dr Rida to take a wife who possessed these qualifications. But he ran away from listening to them whenever they opened up the subject. He would tell them with a smile, "Are you saying what I think you are saying?" Or he would ask them, "But where can I come across a wife of the kind that you describe?"

On the day Ata al-Ayubi persuaded Dr Rida to join the Ministry of Subhi Barakat, the two ladies cried out together, "Now that you have persuaded him to accept a ministerial post, you will be able to persuade him to take a wife!" But Dr Rida laughed, "Where can I come across this woman you describe?"

Several weeks passed before they all met again in their customary evening gatherings. Both men had been buried all the time in their demanding ministerial tasks. When they came together again, the first evening lasted a long time because at the beginning of the evening Dr Rida had said something that surprised them. "I've found her, I've found her!" he proclaimed. At first they thought he had discovered some new scientific theory, and was shouting out like the Greek scholar Archimedes when he cried, "Eureka! Eureka!" on discovering the theory of water pressure. They asked him amid laughter, "What is it you've found?" His face lit up with a broad smile. "I've found what you were looking for. I've found the wife we were wanting!" They almost flew for joy on hearing this wonderful piece of news. The happiest was Ata al-Ayubi when he learnt that the person he was speaking about was from a good family from Lattakia with whom he had long enjoyed a close friendship.

Gradually the picture of what had happened emerged. Earlier one weekday evening when Dr Rida was working in his clinic, the nurse asked if two ladies from a Lattakia family might come in, one of whom needed treatment for her eyes. He said yes and welcomed them. "Which of you is the patient?" he asked. The elder answered with a voice that was firm and confident, "I am, Doctor. My name is Fatima Mamiche. This is my younger sister, Kherié, who has come to be with me. I hope you don't mind her staying here during the consultation." He nodded agreement and asked her to take a seat in the patient's chair, and asked her sister to wait on a leather armchair in a corner of the room. He suggested that while he was treating her sister she might pass the time flicking through the magazines that were scattered on the small table.

When he had completed the examination he went back to the chair at his desk to write out a prescription for drops and some ointment needed by the patient, and to explain how to apply the medication. As he was doing this he noticed that her sister Kherié was totally absorbed in reading a French magazine selected from the Arab and foreign magazines in front of her. Her absorption in reading was contrary to what he expected from patients or those waiting for patients in his clinic. Usually he saw them quickly turning magazine pages and glancing hastily at the illustrations. But she was actually reading a long article with intense interest. What he noticed was her fresh round face with a permanent smile hinting at a soul that was happy and assured. He noticed the elegance of her involvement in the magazine and her gentle way of turning the pages. While he was giving the patient her prescription he said with a smile, "It seems that your sister has been so taken up with reading that she has not noticed that the examination is over!" At this point Kherié became aware and looked up from the magazine, and said apologetically, "I'd like to thank you, doctor, for letting me follow the new instalment of the play of Henry Bataille, *Maman Colibri*, that has been published serially in the magazine *La Théâtre*. The latest issue I found here has not reached us in Lattakia." Dr Rida suggested that she take it so she could finish reading it. She could keep it with her, if she wished, or return it to the clinic when she came back with her sister, who had to make three more visits to follow up the treatment of her eye, which was afflicted with inflammation of the iris.

And so Kherié accompanied her sister each time she came to the clinic. He took care to engage her in conversation, sometimes in Arabic, sometimes in French, trying to discern aspects of her personality and education. He learned that she had graduated from the Carmelite High School in Lattakia. When he asked about her views on drama that she read about in the French magazine, she showed an understanding of the authors' messages, and was capable of analysing the personalities and psychological traits that motivated each of the characters. He observed the bright intelligence that gleamed from her eyes when she spoke at length. Elegant in the way she spoke, she chose her words with care and skill. Her speech hinted at mature reflection and depth of culture and strength of personality. There was also woven into her speech a delicious touch of gentle mockery.

After this prolix description, his friends all saw that the girl had made an impression on him and that she was the right choice. They laughed and said, "You have submitted the girl to as tough an examination as you give to the students at the Medical School." Ata al-Ayubi took up the thread, "You've made a choice, and it is a good choice; the rest will be up to me." He spoke about his connections with the Mamiche family that went back to the time when he was *mutasarrif*, senior civil administrative officer, in Lattakia in Ottoman times. The young girl's father was Khalil Mamiche, a leading figure of the city. He exported goods to Europe and had a number of ships that plied between Lattakia and European ports. He said that in the winter of 1907 a terrible storm had raged over the Mediterranean Sea in which some ships were sunk. God decreed that the ship that had Khalil Mamiche's goods on board be spared, and it reached the port of Lattakia safe and sound. Its arrival coincided with the moment of the birth of his young daughter. He and his wife, Madame Nuzha Harun, agreed to name her Kherié, meaning charity or blessing, seeing her birth as an augury of the safe arrival of the ship. Ata al-Ayubi called to mind this old story when he heard the name Kherié being repeated on his friend's lips.

Ata al-Ayubi added that he was indebted to the Mamiche family for something they had done for him when he was mutasarrif. When he was first appointed to Lattakia there were no hotels or any suitable accommodation as his official residence. On the day after his arrival in the city, Khalil Mamiche and a number of notables called to welcome him. Khalil Mamiche told him that he owned a large house on the beach and that he would be pleased if he would accept it as an official residence for as long as he was in Lattakia. Ata al-Ayubi went on, "My friendship with Khalil Mamiche and his great family goes back to that time. After my posting ended in Lattakia and whenever I went there, I always made sure that Khalil Mamiche was the first of my friends in the city I called on. Similarly he always makes a point of calling on me whenever he comes to Damascus – and that as soon as he arrives. Tomorrow I'll get in touch with him and ask for his daughter's hand for our dear friend, hoping that God will see it as a good omen for him and his family just as He made her a good omen for her father on the day of her birth."

Just one week after the wedding between Dr Rida and

Kherié Mamiche on 17 July 1925, neighbours and friends called to be introduced the bride. When they met her they realised that she exceeded all they could imagine or expect from descriptions that they had heard of the long-awaited bride.

Within a few days this pretty bride from Lattakia entered the hearts not just of near neighbours but all the women of Damascus who came to congratulate and welcome her. The elegance of her talk sparkled and captivated. They were amazed at how good she was at talking with everyone, whatever their age or intellectual powers, with old, young and very young. When she engaged in conversation with someone it was as if she had known them for a very long time. She would steer the conversation and turn her smiling face to them, and listen to them with ear, with eye and with heart. Each would think Kherié Saïd was interested in them and nobody else. Moreover, she had a playful humour and sweet raillery that made people devoted to her.

After the period when people called to meet her and congratulate her, Kherié threw herself into reorganising the beautiful home. She made herself familiar with every part of the house, every piece of furniture, and every nook of the garden surrounding the house, giving them all a new spark and a touch of refined taste. Her charming work also impacted on the way Dr Rida looked. A serene contentment brightened his life.

Day by day, a friendship with Madame Adila grew, and in time she showed interest in public work, and a desire to take a public role that would complement her husband's activities in the university, education and public health. When Madame Adila told her all she aimed to do in educational and social spheres, Kherié showed great enthusiasm and asked her to count on her as her chief helper in all the projects she could think of.

The two of them sat down and made plans first of all to set up an educational foundation that specialised in establishing a national school for girls that would be of a standard, in terms of pedagogy and culture, as good as any foreign or missionary schools in Damascus. In this proposed school the Syrian girls would learn nationalist principles, Arabic, the basics of religion and other subjects, foreign languages, the fine arts – drawing, music and crafts practised by women – with the best teachers, men and women, Syrian and Lebanese. They drew in outstanding and well-educated women to take part in this project of establishing the school, which they named *Duha al-Adab*, meaning The Spreading Tree of Culture. It was launched in 1928 and was indeed a pioneering school in every meaning of the word. It soon filled a huge gap in educational life, and its distinguished graduates contributed to the emancipation of women in Syria later. Madame Kherié was one of the most active of the members working in the society and her enthusiasm for work was shown in her attendance at all the weekly committee meetings. If she had to travel, as soon as she was back in Damascus, she renewed her activity and briefed herself about every detail of the society and the school, great and small, until she was satisfied. She took the initiative in harnessing the resources of the society to support the national movement in its demand for independence, and collected money to support the families of those who had been arrested by the Mandate authorities or of those who had gone on strike in protest.

As well as working for societies such as *Duha al-Adab*, she also joined social and existing humanitarian groups such as the *Jami'a Nuqta al-Halib*, The Drop of Milk Society, founded in 1922. This dealt with issues relating to children, spreading an awareness of infant care, the treatment of sick children and the distribution of pasteurised milk to children in need and of medicines to the sick. She was one of the most prominent of the founders of *al-Is'af al-'Am al-Nisa'i*, Women's General First Aid, which concerned itself with treating the poor in private clinics and the inoculation of children, and providing nourishing food and clothing, especially during winter. Among the important national projects in which she worked with Madame Adila and other committed friends was the Society for the Advancement of Syrian Women, which had been founded during the Faisal era. Among its leading aims were the revival of traditional crafts such as cashmere weaving, copperware and mosaics, and raising awareness of these among the general public with annual exhibitions. It also found employment for needy women in their own homes so they could bring in some income to help bear life's burdens, especially if they had lost the breadwinner of the household.

It was Madame Kherié who had the idea of developing the

—

manufacture of embroidered cashmere. This had been a kind of cloth only used for the material tied round the tarbushes of men of religion, sheikhs and those merchants in the souk who still wore traditional dress. (These were known then as Lam-Alif wraps, from the way they draped around a head in the shape of the Arabic letters Lam and Alif.) She saw that, in order to popularise this attractive local work, they could also be made into tablecloths that could replace those that were foreign imports. This original idea of Madame Kherié was a key feature in the manufacture of cashmere cloth, and its production saw a great boom. These Syrian tablecloths became beautiful presents that visitors to Syria, Arab and foreign, took with them when they returned home. Syrians were proud of them and sent them to friends abroad. The Society for the Advancement of Syrian Women also arranged weekly lectures with the aim of increasing cultural and scientific awareness among women. Madame Kherié asked her husband to provide the society with university staff to take part in carrying out this fine mission.

She was also in the forefront of those taking part in Syrian and Arab women's conferences held in Damascus, Beirut or Cairo. She took the lead in humanitarian initiatives, collecting funds for the victims of disasters such as floods, earthquakes and fires that had taken place in sister Arab countries. She volunteered to be among missions that went to those countries to succour the victims and distribute assistance.

After she returned from her travels she liked to describe

to her friends in her agreeable way what she saw in the countries of the West and what it was possible to borrow from them to develop and encourage the work of the societies. Or she would tell delightful and instructive anecdotes. One example happened at a dinner party. She had been invited with her husband, in his capacity as Principal of the Syrian University, to attend the celebrations marking the four-hundredth anniversary of the Collège de France. She spoke about this at a dinner party after her return. She related that she and her husband were staying in the Lutetia Hotel in Paris. She went on to say, "We were surprised to receive an invitation to have dinner with His Majesty King Faisal I, King of Iraq, who was on a private visit to Paris and staying at the same hotel. My husband was very happy to receive this invitation for it enabled him to meet again the King whom he had first met in Aleppo thirteen years earlier, when he gave Dr Rida the task of reopening the Medical School in Damascus. After that the Allies went back on the undertakings they had made to his father, Sharif Husain. The French had then come, abolished the Faisal monarchy in Syria, and forced him to leave.

"But the big surprise was when the Secretary General of the French Ministry for Foreign Affairs, Philippe Berthelot,[43] who had also been invited to the dinner party, actually said, 'Let us drink to the health of His Majesty King Faisal... King of Syria and Iraq.' My husband leaned over to me and whispered in my ear, 'It seems that the French have regretted the crimes they committed against the rights of the King, for here we have them acknowledging now that he was King of Syria. But this repentance comes, alas, too late.'"

Sunday, 30 June 1935

Almost one week after the conclusion of the Annual Conference of the Egyptian Medical Society, which had been held in Damascus, Dr Rida Saïd received a telegram he had been expecting from the Chairman of the Conference, the distinguished doctor Ali Pasha Ibrahim, informing him that Egypt had decided to recognise the diplomas of the Arab Medical School in Damascus.

The path to achieving this recognition had been long and demanding. The story began when the first International Conference for Tropical Diseases took place in Cairo in 1928. Dr Rida represented Syria as Dean of the School of Medicine together with Dr Ahmad Hamdi al-Khayyat and Dr Trabaud, professors at the School. He found this a convenient opportunity to put on display the writings on medicine that had been published by the School of Medicine to prove that Arabic was an appropriate language for medical literature.

Things turned out as planned, for the writings brought along by the Syrian delegation won the admiration and appreciation of the Egyptians. Indeed they were amazed that it had been possible for the Syrian doctors to mould the Arabic language to the literature of complex scientific researches. The Egyptian newspaper *al-Muqattam*, in one of its leading articles, praised what the Syrian Medical School had done, believing that it had achieved the impossible.

"The School of Medicine in Damascus," it went on to say, "has brought us fresh proof that the teaching of medicine in Arabic is possible. It has proved this contention with a collection of valuable books written by the staff of this school. It has performed a majestic service for the Arabic language.[44] It might be that what the Medical School in Damascus has done is an example to be emulated..."

A few years later he relinquished the post of Principal of the Syrian University, following his departure from the Deanship of the Medical School in 1932. He took advantage of the reception given to the writings of the school at that conference in Cairo and consulted with his colleague, the new Dean, Professor Dr Ahmad Munif al-A'idi.[45] They would take a decisive step to have the diploma of the Arab Medical School recognised in Egypt and other Arab countries.

Dr al-A'idi suggested that they get in touch with the Egyptian Medical Society, inviting it to hold its next conference in Damascus, and that its members, who were very distinguished Egyptian medical professors, make themselves familiar with the experiment of teaching medicine through the medium of Arabic while they attended the conference. Dr Rida Saïd and Dr al-A'idi agreed that the invitation should be sent in the name of the Syrian Surgical Medicine Society of which they were both founding members. That society soon held an extraordinary meeting to discuss arranging the invitation and organisational matters for the conference if it was to be held in Damascus. Dr al-A'idi was chosen unanimously to travel to Cairo and present officially to the Egyptian Medical Society the invitation to them to hold this (its eighth) conference in Damascus in June 1935.

The task given to Dr al-A'idi was delicate and sensitive because the Egyptians, who at that time taught medicine through the medium of English, were sceptical of the value of teaching it in Arabic. But Dean al-A'idi succeeded in his mission, thanks to his tactful and intelligent way of discussing things, his eloquence and his firm belief that Arabic should be the language in which the sciences were taught, a belief that had not wavered since he took part in the foundation of the Arab Medical School.

There were close links between the family of Dr al-A'idi and a number of distinguished Egyptian families, most notably the famous Abaza family (among whom was Dr Mahmud Sulaiman Abaza, a member of the Egyptian Medical Society). These connections played a role with all those with whom he talked.

Accordingly the conference took place in Damascus between 22 and 27 June 1935. A comprehensive official programme included plenty of scientific sessions and visits as well as outings to tourist sites. The opening session was held in the auditorium of the Syrian University[46] under the auspices of the President of the Republic, Muhammad Ali al-Abid.

In his capacity as Principal of the University, Dr Rida gave an eloquent speech in which he welcomed his Egyptian colleagues. Dr Munif al-A'idi did the same in his capacity as Dean of the Arab Medical School. The reply was given by the President of the Egyptian Medical Society and Chairman of the conference, Dr Ali Pasha Ibrahim, in an impassioned speech full of national feeling.

The *Journal of the Arab Medical School* reported the events of the conference and described the exceptionally friendly reception given to the Egyptian guests in Damascus. The *Journal* also published reports of the sessions and focused on the Egyptian professors' presence at the medicine classes given in Arabic, how they tested the students' knowledge and to what extent they had benefited from what they had heard, and how much they had absorbed from lectures given in fluent classical Arabic. These professors moved from one row to another in the Medical School in order to sit next to the students and listen to the lectures given by the Syrian medical staff. Day by day they became more persuaded of the success of the Syrian experiment. The conference ended with the Egyptians recognising the qualification of the Arab Medical College in Damascus, and soon other Arab countries followed in Egypt's steps in recognising the school's qualification. After that Arab countries short of doctors preferred to engage doctors who had graduated from the Damascus School.

Sunday, 21 April 1940

On this day Dr Rida Saïd accepted an invitation to a dinner hosted by the Dean of the Faculty of Medicine Dr Husni Sabah,[47] at the Orient Palace Hotel, in honour of a visiting Turkish medical delegation led by the chemist Mustafa Bey. He had first tried to decline the invitation but his old student Dr Sabah insisted. That and his friendship with the guest of honour made him change his mind.

He was feeling exhausted after a full day's work at his clinic. When he came home he would have preferred to go to bed and rest. The numbness that he had felt in his left hand ten weeks earlier had recurred. When his wife came in to see how he was, he reassured her by saying all was as it should be. He asked her about the children. She said that Adnan, when he came from the clinic, had gone out with Rafic and his friend Adil al-Hanbali. As for Omayma, Houzama and Racha, they had gone to have a rest. But sleep had eluded Wafic. He asked her to bring Wafic to him so he could soothe him. She brought him in and he cuddled him, kissing him on both cheeks. His mother then took him and rocked him until he dozed off and she took him back to where he slept.

Only four months had passed since Wafic was born. His arrival brought enormous joy to them both, for he was the last of their offspring. God had decreed that after three daughters, they were blessed with this good-looking child, who was a source of great happiness to his parents, to his stepbrothers and all his sisters.

This overwhelming happiness was the outcome of the

conscious way Madame Kherié brought the children up and managed the family. From the time she married she regarded Adnan and Rafic as her own actual children, as no less a part of her tasks, managing their lives at home and at school. After she was blessed with Omayma, Houzama and Racha, these girls responded to the idea that Adnan and Rafic were their elder brothers and they dealt with them with love and respect.

One event is remembered which was a great shock to the family. It took place on the day after Adnan graduated from the Medical School,[48] when the outbreak of the Second World War prevented him from travelling to France to specialise in ophthalmology. He had packed his bags for the journey on the day war broke out, 1 September 1939. He was disappointed, distressed and depressed at seeing the golden opportunity slip from his grasp. He stayed in his room and would not come out, unable to look at his packed bags or at the ticket which he had for a few days seen as the way to happiness and hope. But it was now more like an announcement of death, the death of the dreams he had been living for. He no longer knew what to do.

The family did their utmost to lighten his distress. His mother said to him tenderly, "What's happened to you, my dear son, is not the end of the world. You must praise Allah that you are not leaving your home, and that what happens to you will not be what will happen to many of your contemporaries who reached Europe just before the outbreak of war there. Today lines of communications have been cut, and none but God knows when they'll be able to come back home. You should bear in mind the verse of the Holy Qur'an, *It may happen that ye hate a thing which is good for you.*[49] Perhaps God Almighty has prevented you from going in order to offer you something better, and dearer to your heart. Do not fret about something that has eluded you. The Sufi imams have a lovely term that expresses the meaning. 'Perhaps He gives you something in order to prevent you from something; perhaps He prevents you from something in order to give you something else.'"

At this point his father came into Adnan's room. "I've heard, my dear boy, what Lady Kherié has told you," he said. "I'd like to add: The fact that you can't travel to specialise because of this emergency is undoubtedly important, but the opportunity for practical experience now open to you is no less important. There are several choices that I see open to you to gain this necessary professional medical experience. For example, you can work in my clinic, or you can go, as some of your colleagues have done, to another Arab country that insists on asking for Syrian doctors to work there. I understand from your friend and fellow graduate Dr Muwaffaq al-Maliki that he is thinking of doing just this. The third choice is to open a private clinic. You can opt for one of these courses of action until the war is over. God has created what you do not know. Get up and don't be so sad. There is no way out of this depression unless you take the initiative and put right out of your mind this matter of the cancellation of going to Paris. It's part of the inevitable destiny of war that affects not just you, but the whole of mankind. You must make a decision that you're comfortable with and move on with the blessing of God."

Adnan's features relaxed. He unpacked his bags and started to contemplate another new day. A few days later he informed his parents that he had decided to give up the idea of going to another Arab country. He was thinking of working for a year or two in his father's clinic and gaining some experience. He would then open up a private clinic, not in Damascus, but in provincial Syria where there was an urgent need for ophthalmologists who were young new graduates.

Dr Rida was delighted with his son's decision. After he had retired as Principal of the Syrian University at the beginning of 1936 at his own request, patients thronged to his clinic, from which he was often called away by important official responsibilities. He therefore saw that Adnan at his side would relieve some of the burden of treating the huge numbers. He never liked turning any of them away disappointed, especially if they were poor. They would come and see him on Thursdays, which he put aside for giving free treatment. He thought that if Adnan worked with him under his direction this would give him more excellent practical experience. He would need this when he opened his own private clinic.[50] His choice of opening a clinic far from Damascus was another reason for Dr Rida's quiet satisfaction on hearing of this decision. Ever since he had taken on important positions, a major priority was the promotion of a public awareness of health throughout Syria, especially in the rural areas of Syria where there was a shortage of doctors. Instead charlatans and swindlers claiming some knowledge of medicine were used by rural people seeking a cure, but the result of it all was that their health got worse and disease spread.[51]

His mother was no less delighted by what Adnan had made up his mind to do. She was so happy to see one of her family who had reached maturity and had learnt how to feel his way and find his own footing, and was the model of his father.

Madame Kherié was the lady in charge of the house just as she was the lady in charge of her community. All her many social and humanitarian activities and commitments did not divert her for one moment from her total commitment to bringing up their children and listening to their joys and sorrows. She was equally committed to ensuring that her husband had his rest and looking after the social demands of his work that required hosting a number of receptions and dinner parties at home. She was noted for her elegance and good management. Her relationship with her husband was marked by love and mutual respect. Ever since they got married she addressed him as "Dr Rida Bey." In return he always called her "Lady Kherié." Out of respect she used to refrain from smoking in his presence. She tried to persuade herself that he did not know that she smoked in secret or, when he was at home, out of doors. But when once he had to stay at home for the whole day, he called her. "Lady Kherié," he said, "I know you smoke, so do bring your cigarette box for, I think, you need one!"

The loveliest feature in their relationship was that remarkable harmony in their thoughts and behaviour. Each told the other whatever was on their minds and what they wanted to accomplish, he in the university and she in the field of her humanitarian and social concerns. He was proud of these and was always encouraging her, seeing her as an ideal companion for him in the jobs he took on.

He believed his marriage to Kherié Mamiche was effectively his third and final return to his homeland.

He remembered one day in 1929 when he was full of anxiety. The building of the university auditorium for which he had worked so hard was within sight of completion. The famous calligrapher Mamduh al-Shahir pressed him to provide some words that he wanted to place at the entrance outside the auditorium so he could write them in Kufic script.

For a number of days he looked for the ideally appropriate words that would encapsulate the meaning and mission of the university. It should in due course be the motto that would be at the head of all publications, correspondence and diplomas. This is what Western universities did, each one choosing its own motto, written in the ancient Latin language.

On one of those nerve-wracking days when he was anxious about dozens of available options from traditional Arabic precepts, but he had not found one that gave him complete satisfaction. The architect and the calligrapher were insisting on a motto, which he was having such difficulty finding.

Madame Kherié came to soothe him. "It's easy to write a long speech!" he told her, "But as for one sentence which we want it to be short, eloquent and comprehensive, we find one of them suggests many meanings – this just aggravates the difficulty and it becomes hard to resolve!" Madame Kherié brought him a copy of the Holy Qur'an and said he should read some chapters, *suras*. Perhaps God would open his heart and ease the problem of finding the words. Half an hour later he cried out joyfully, calling his wife in to give her the good news that God had provided him with just the words he wanted. They came from Surat Ta Ha. He sent for the calligrapher Mamduh and told him his choice. A few days later the builders raised the marble slab on which Mamduh had inscribed the blessed verse, the *aya*, and installed it above the stone façade of the main entrance. The aya consisted of four eloquent words, encouraging mankind to seek knowledge and to expand that knowledge:

waqul rabbi zidni 'ilman

Say: My Lord! Increase me in knowledge.[52]

Thursday, 31 May 1945

His eyes were closed and he was trying to doze off, but in vain. When he heard the voice of his doctor, Eli Na'man, talking to Lady Kherié, he opened his eyes a little and could make out his beloved doctor sitting at his bedside. He was not expecting him to come today after having been away for three consecutive days. During this time he had been continuing to follow his course of treatment prescribed since the latest medical crisis. He had been full of anxiety while his doctor was away. He had heard the sound of distant explosions and of constant gunfire throughout these days. But nobody in the house wanted to tell him what was going on in the city; he felt they were deliberately concealing what was happening from him.

"I've been worried about you, Doctor. What's prevented you from coming since Monday last? I want you to tell me what's going on in the country. They're hiding it from me, and not telling me anything. For Heaven's sake tell me what's going on there and what they're hiding from me."

"I'll tell you everything, but to calm you down, first take a spoonful of this new medicine I've brought."

He got Dr Rida to sit up in bed so he could take the medicine.

"I was afraid something terrible had happened to you, God forbid, and this had kept you from coming to see me. Now tell me, what exactly has been going on?"

"I'll tell you everything. Terrible things have happened. But we praise God that the worst ended quickly, and there is nothing more to worry about.

"Thirteen days ago, that is, on 18 May," he went on, "the French High Commissioner, General Beynet, demanded from the national government that emerged from the 1943 elections agreement to three items: the independence of French cultural institutions in Syria; the protection of

French economic interests; and acceptance of the establishment of French naval and air bases on Syrian soil."

Dr Rida became somewhat agitated and turned to the doctor.

"But they are items that are incompatible with Syrian independence," he said, "independence that has been recognised by the Great Powers as well as France herself. General Catroux announced, in the name of General De Gaulle, complete Syrian independence in leaflets dropped by French aeroplanes on Damascus on 8 June 1941. General Catroux confirmed this declaration on 27 September that year with his written statement that included the call, 'Long live independent Syria, long live France!' He supported this recognition by inviting Syria last month to attend the San Francisco Conference that set up the United Nations Organisation."

"...Of course, Syria did not agree to these unjustified French demands. When the government presented the proposed items to the Syrian Parliament last Saturday, 26 May, they were rejected without question. The following day, there were large popular demonstrations hostile to France and these demands. But Damascus was shocked by a fresh French provocation when they sent troops of Senegalese soldiers into the streets of the city. But the worst is what happened on Tuesday evening, 29 May, when French soldiers stormed the Parliament building on the orders of General Oliva Roger, after it was shelled. The Parliament's police station was destroyed on the grounds that the police disregarded orders to salute the French flag that had been raised on the

French military post opposite the Parliament building. The Senegalese soldiers were not satisfied with just killing thirty policemen, but they cut up their bodies and mutilated the corpses. The French bombardment continued in different quarters of the city, causing hundreds of civilian casualties – dead and wounded. The bombardment only stopped today, on the third day, as a result of a strongly worded British ultimatum sent to the French government."

"*La hawla wa-la quwata illa bi'llah*, There is no strength and no power save with God. What have the French learned from the lessons of the past? How could they have insisted on sending these stupid soldiers to our country to behave in this barbaric fashion? Have they not been persuaded that France, after the Second World War, and its terrible defeat, is no longer the great power that it has been in the past?

"Now, Dr Eli, please tell me honestly. Has the university suffered any damage? I hope none of the staff or students have been harmed during these events."

"I can reassure you: the university and its buildings have not been damaged. And I have not heard that any of the staff or students have come to any harm, but the huge loss has been the killing of our colleague Dr Muslim al-Barudi while he was carrying out his duty in tending to the victims of the bombardment. French snipers deliberately fired at the white ambulance transporting casualties, destroying it. It killed Dr Muslim at once in Hijaz Station Square."

"*Rahmat Allah alaih*, May God have mercy on him. They have ended the life of a man of duty."

Dr Rida's voice trembled as he recalled to mind his medical colleague and the other martyrs who died defending the freedom of their country and muttered hoarsely, "You can be sure, Dr Eli, that the blood of these martyrs will be the last innocent blood to be shed in our country for the sake of independence. The French occupation will pass away, just as I have always said it would. The barbaric shelling of our beloved Damascus has done more harm to France than it has done to us. Their remaining in our homeland has reached the end of its course. They will be here for only a few more days. The whole world supports our independence and it will not be possible for a handful of stupid Frenchmen to isolate us as they did after the Battle of Maysalun."

He rested his head back on the pillow and dozed off.

A Final Page

In 1945 an expatriate intellectual of Syrian origin launched a magazine in Brazil with a new vision and programme. He wanted it to convey to his readers a more contemporary picture of developments and achievements witnessed in the lands of the Arab mother countries in culture, economics, industry and education. He did not want their knowledge of the Arab homeland to be based on a misty folkloric nostalgia that did not go beyond repetition of memories of the past. The magazine was given the name *The New Homeland*, and it was decided that his first journalistic assignment would deal with Syria, his country of origin, and that he would look first at the Syrian University that had grown up and flourished at the hands of its founder and Principal, and Dean of the Medical School, for over sixteen years: Dr Rida Saïd.[53]

He intended to have a series of interviews with Dr Rida Saïd that would gather data about the university and the personality of its Principal, whose name was linked to its foundation, its development and its expansion. He knew that the name of Dr Rida Saïd had been involved with the launching of medical, social and educational initiatives that he had promoted and taken part in, such as the project for bringing the waters of Ain al-Fijja to Damascus houses, and introducing the baccalaureate to Syria when he was Minister of Education. To his dismay the journalist, when he reached Damascus, learned that Dr Rida Saïd was ill in bed. His wife, Madame Kherié Saïd, apologised and said the interviews he wanted would not be possible. But she told the journalist politely that her husband, anyway, was far too modest to talk at length about his many achievements or boast about them. She therefore advised him to interview a number of her husband's friends, colleagues and students, who had known him at close quarters and from whom he could obtain a completely accurate and vivid picture of the man and his achievements. She added that she hoped, after these interviews, that her husband's health would have improved and that he would then be happy to meet him and talk to him.

The journalist took Madame Kherié's advice, and at once got in touch with people over the course of a month, until he had gathered plenty of information. When his visit was near its end, Dr Rida Saïd was still bedridden, still fighting his long and painful illness. Not wanting to burden him with a long conversation, the journalist asked Madame Kherié if he could call for just a few minutes so he could meet him face to face after having learnt so much about him.

The Brazilian journalist wrote about his meeting with the founder of the Syrian University, Dr Rida Saïd, on 26 October 1945.

Madame Kherié Saïd was good nature and consideration personified. When I told her I would be leaving two days later, going back to Brazil, she did not want to go back on the promise she had made, and she would allow me to interview her husband after I had completed the interviews with his friends and colleagues. But she beseeched me – and clear signs of anxiety were etched on her face – to restrict my talk with him as much as possible, because he was exhausted from the illness he was struggling with. I promised that I would do that. She showed me into the room where he lay half-asleep. She told him I was there. He opened his eyes slowly and welcomed me in a faint voice, and thanked me with words that I could hardly make out in spite of all my efforts.

"I don't wish to burden you," I said. "I am very happy to have the honour of meeting you after having heard so much about you and of the many wonderful things you have achieved. But one question has pressed itself on me, and I would like to hear an answer to it from yourself before I return home.

"Your life has been crowded with pioneering activities that should be recorded in memoirs written by yourself. Have you thought of doing this?"

He shook his head, and a faint smile appeared on his lips, but it was no less a smile full of sweetness.

"There's nothing I want to hide!" he whispered.

And he dropped off to sleep.

The journalist went on to say on the last page:

On 28 October 1945 I was leaving Damascus by car. All the time I was unable to stop going over those few remarkable words that Dr Rida Saïd had whispered: "There's nothing I want to hide." He knew that people wrote their memoirs in order to hide more than they chose to remember.

We drove along by the university buildings and I noticed that the Syrian flag was at half-mast. I asked the driver what it meant.

"This morning," he said, "they announced the death of the founder of the Syrian University ... and the city is in mourning."

TIMELINE FOR THE LIFE OF RIDA SAÏD AND CONTEMPORARY HISTORICAL EVENTS

1876

11 April

Birth of Rida Saïd in Damascus.

30 May

Deposition of the Ottoman Sultan Abdul Aziz and accession of Sultan Murad V.

1 August

Removal of Sultan Murad V on the grounds of alleged disorders in his mental faculties, and accession of his half-brother, Sultan Abdul Hamid II.

19 December

Proclamation of the Basic Law, the Constitution.

1877

10 January

Death of Madame Khadija al-Muradi, the mother of Rida Saïd, during the governorship of Umar Fawzi Pasha, which lasts only eight days.

14 January

Sitting of the first Ottoman Parliament in Istanbul, the Assembly of Notables, and the Representative Assembly, in the presence of Sultan Abdul Hamid, who is upset by speeches of the delegates as they call for a limit to the absolute powers of the Sultan and emphasise the competence of the Representative Assembly and demand that he rule constitutionally.

1878

14 February

Sultan Abdul Hamid's disapproval of the Representatives leads to him issuing an imperial decree dissolving the Assembly and ordering the exile from Istanbul of the Liberals of the country, at the head of whom is the former Grand Vizier, Midhat Pasha, known as the Father of the Constitution.

The Governor of Syria at this time is Ahmad Jawdat (Cevdet) Pasha, whose governorship lasts nine months and three days. He is succeeded by the exiled Midhat Pasha, whose governorship lasts one year, eight months and ten days. He is one of the most important Governors of Syria. He carries out many important reforms such as the foundation of the School of Crafts. He collects books for the General Public Library, *Dar al-Kutub*, in al-Zahiriya. He opens the souk that has his name and extends many of the streets of Damascus. He encourages the foundation of cultural, social and educational societies, such as the Maqasid Charitable Society in Beirut. He also encourages the fine arts. To the young artist, musician, actor and playwright Ahmad al-Kabbani Abu Khalil, he gives a grant amounting to 900 golden pounds to cover the costs of putting on a theatrical performance.

1879

Second governorship of Ahmad Hamdi (his first was in 1875) starts. He is appointed Governor of Syria after Midhat Pasha is removed and banished. During his governorship, which lasts five years and fourteen days, a decree from the Sublime Porte is issued forbidding Ahmad al-Kabbani from continuing his acting in Damascus. He is forced to go to Egypt in 1884 and works there for sixteen years at the Opera House and at other theatres in Egyptian cities.

1880

In order to strengthen his mother tongue, Rida Saïd learns the basics of reading, writing, arithmetic and religious studies at the al-Shabikaliya Qur'anic school in the Qanawat quarter, studying under a private teacher of Arabic in the house.

1884

Rida Saïd enters the elementary division of the Rushdiya Military School during the second governorship of Rashid Nashid Pasha, which lasts for two years and five months. During his time, Souk Hamidiya is opened. While he is studying at the Rushdiya Military School his father arranges for him to have a private teacher for Arabic, Lieutenant Abdul Rahman, and another for the French language, Yuzbashi Umar Lutfi.

1885

Rida Saïd's father, General Muhammad Saïd, asks to be transferred from his field work in the cavalry division to a desk job at army headquarters.

1887

Rida Saïd ends his time in the elementary division of the Rushdiya Military School; he is eleven years old.

1888

Rida Saïd's father sends him to Istanbul, in spite of his youth – he is twelve years old – and enrols him in the preparatory division attached to the Military Medical School, where he lives as a boarder.

1896

After completing his studies in the preparatory division Rida Saïd joins the Military Medical School in Istanbul.

1898

Visit of the German Kaiser Wilhelm II to Damascus.

1902

11 September
Rida Saïd graduates from the Military Medical School with a qualification as doctor-surgeon.

17 November

He is appointed to the rank of yuzbashi doctor in Istanbul.

1903

27 September

Opening of the Turkish Medical School in Damascus.

18 November

Appointment of Rida Saïd as Doctor-Chemist at the Customs Department, Trabzon/Trebizond.

1904

4 April

Abolition of his post as Doctor-Chemist at Trabzon/Trebizond and the transfer of Rida Saïd to Istanbul and appointment as Doctor-Surgeon at Gulhane Hospital.

1905

Retirement of his father, Governor Muhammad Saïd, from his military work.

1906

Appointment of Rida Saïd as Assistant to the Ophthalmology Section in the Military Medical School.

1907

General As'ad Pasha, Professor of Ophthalmology in the Military Medical School, appoints him as his assistant.

1908

Rida Saïd raised to the rank of Kul ağasi (major).

1909

27 April

Deposition of Sultan Abdul Hamid II after a reign of thirty-three years, and the accession of Sultan Muhammad V in his place.

Rida Saïd is sent to Paris to specialise in ophthalmology at the Hôtel-Dieu Hospital attached to the Paris College of Medicine.

1911

19 January

Wedding of Rida Saïd and the pharmacist Marcelle Holbe in Paris.

15 June

Graduation at Hôtel-Dieu and the award of a Certificate of Specialisation in Ophthalmology and Eye Surgery from the Paris College of Medicine.

30 June

He leaves Paris for Istanbul with his wife, Marcelle, and her grandmother, Eugénie.

15 July

He returns to his former post in the Military Medical School.

1912

18 October

Outbreak of the Balkan War. Rida Saïd takes part in it with the medical relief team in the field hospital at the front.

1913

16 April

End of military operations.

1 May

Return of Rida Saïd from the war front to Istanbul.

13 May

His meeting with his old teacher Yuzbashi Umar Lutfi.

1 June

Birth of his son Adnan in Istanbul.

1 August

Issue of the decree transferring Rida Saïd to the Military Hospital in Damascus with a group of his Arab fellow doctors. He comes to Damascus with his wife, Marcelle, her grandmother, Eugénie, and his son, Adnan.

1914

3 August

Start of the First World War in Europe.

4 August

Transfer of Rida Saïd to the post of Director of the Medical

Board of the Hijaz Railway, where he becomes a civilian for the first time.

28 October

Entry of Turkey into the war on Germany's side.

10 November

Death of the father of Rida Saïd, General Muhammad Saïd.

5 December

Arrival in Damascus of Jamal Pasha as Governor of Syria and the start of a series of disasters – famine, epidemics, confiscations, compulsory military purchases for the front etc.

1916

6 May

Jamal Pasha sentences twenty-one men from the Arab Liberal Party to death in Damascus and Beirut.

16 May

Signing of the Sykes-Picot Agreement by Britain and France that will partition the remains of the Ottoman state after the end of the war.

9 June

Sharif Husain proclaims the Arab Revolt against the Turks.

1917

15 March

Birth of Rida Saïd's second son, Rafic, in Damascus.

July

Election of Rida Saïd as head of the Damascus Municipality.

November

Removal of Jamal Pasha from Syria and his transfer to Istanbul.

1918

8 January

President of the United States, Woodrow Wilson, announces to Congress his Fourteen Points for a just and lasting peace.

3 July

Sultan Muhammad VI succeeds Sultan Muhammad V.

3 October

Triumphant entry of Prince Faisal bin al-Husain into Damascus at the head of his Arab forces.

7 October

French naval forces land at Beirut.

30 October

Illness of Rida Saïd's wife, Marcelle, with typhoid fever and Rida Saïd's decision to accompany her to France via Aleppo and Istanbul.

6 November

Visit of Prince Faisal to Aleppo.

18 November

Death of the wife of Rida Saïd in Aleppo and her burial there.

9 November

Meeting with Prince Faisal in the Baron Hotel where Rida Saïd is charged with reopening the Medical School in Damascus.

12 November

He leaves Aleppo with his two sons, Adnan and Rafic, and their great-grandmother.

14 November

Their arrival in Damascus.

14 November

Meeting with the Governor, General Rida Pasha al-Rikabi, to prepare the opening of the Arab Medical School to replace the Turkish Medical School.

22 November

Prince Faisal travels to the Peace Conference held in Paris.

1919

12 January

Opening of the Arab Medical School in Damascus and the appointment of Dr Rida Saïd as its Dean and Professor of Ophthalmology.

18 January

Opening of the Peace Conference in Paris.

29 January

Prince Faisal gives a speech at the Conference.

May

The King-Crane Commission travels to embark on the fact-finding mission entrusted to them by President Wilson.

3 May

Return of Prince Faisal to Damascus from Europe.

2 July

Holding of the Syrian National Congress in Damascus.

28 August

Publication of the report by the King-Crane Commission making it clear that Syria prefers an American mandate in the event of it not getting independence.

13 September

Return of Prince Faisal once again to Europe.

25 September

Opening of the School of Law in Damascus and the appointment of Abdul Latif Salah as its Dean.

8 October

Appointment of General Gouraud as French High Commissioner in Syria and Commander of the Army of the Levant. His declaration before he leaves Paris that he will impose the French Mandate on Syria and Lebanon.

18 November

Arrival of Gouraud in Lebanon.

1920

16 January

Return of Prince Faisal from Europe to Damascus.

18 January

Defeat of Georges Clemenceau in elections, to be replaced by Alexandre Millerand as Prime Minister.

8 March

The Syrian National Congress declares the independence of Syria and the appointment of Prince Faisal as its King.

25 April

Signing of the San Remo Resolution between France and Britain authorising their mandates over Syria, Lebanon, Palestine and Iraq.

14 July

Gouraud sends an ultimatum to King Faisal telling him he must accept the French Mandate over Syria.

24 July

Battle of Maysalun between the French Army advancing to occupy Damascus and the remnants of the Arab forces that were routed because of their vulnerability in facing the huge invading army. The martyrdom of the Minister of Defence, General Yusuf al-Azma, who was commanding the Arab forces.

25 July

Entry of the French forces into Damascus and the start of
the French occupation of Syria.

28 July

King Faisal leaves Syria.

15 August

Appointment of Professor Abdul Qadir al-Azm as Dean of
the School of Law.

31 August

Gouraud's edict establishing the state of Greater Lebanon
containing four *qada*s (administrative districts) – Hasbiya,
Rashaya, al-Biqa' and Ba'lbak) – that are detached from
Syria.

1 September

Rida Saïd meets the Gouraud's Delegate in Syria, Georges
Catroux.

1923

9 May

Appointment of General Maxime Weygand as French High
Commissioner, replacing General Gouraud.

15 June

Decree founding the Syrian University is issued in Damascus when Subhi Barakat is Prime Minister of the united Syrian states, and receives the ratification of General Weygand.

29 September

Mandate law becomes operative in Syria and Lebanon.

1 October

Election of Dr Rida Saïd as Principal of the Syrian University as well as being Dean of the Arab Medical School.

1924

1 January

Publication of the first issue of the *Journal of the Arab Medical School*.

23 February

Publication of the concession for the project of supply of water from Ain al-Fijja to the residences of Damascus, authorised with the signature of General Weygand.

20 December

Appointment of Dr Rida Saïd as Minister of Education in the government of Subhi Barakat.

1925

2 January

Appointment of General Sarrail as High Commissioner, replacing General Weygand.

17 July

Wedding of Dr Rida Saïd to Miss Kherié Khalil Mamiche.

18 July

Start of the Syrian Revolt in Jabal Druze.

20 July

Rebels, under the leadership of Sultan Pasha al-Atrash, occupy Salkhad.

22 July

Defeat of the expeditionary force of Colonel Norman at the town of al-Kafir.

3 August

Failure of the Michaud campaign in al-Mazra'a.

12 October

Revolt reaches Damascus.

20 October

French shelling of Damascus concentrated on the Citadel of
Damascus and the Citadel of Mezze and the destruction of
a large part of the city.

10 November

Appeal of General Sarrail to France after the protest of
a group of French Members of Parliament who demand
his removal because of his foolhardy conduct by shelling
Damascus.

2 December

Appointment of Count Henri de Jouvenel in place of
General Sarrail and his arrival in Beirut.

3 December

Resignation of the government of Subhi Barakat.

1926

11 February

Return of Rida Saïd to his post as Principal of the Syrian
University after the end of his ministerial role.

2 May

Formation of the government of Damad Ahmad Nami.

De Jouvenel and Catroux visit the Medical School and the Syrian University, escorted by Dr Rida Saïd, Principal of the University.

June

Resignation of Count de Jouvenel because the French government does not agree to his project of cooperation with the Syrian nationalists.

3 September

Appointment of Henri Ponsot, a senior official of the French Ministry for Foreign Affairs, as High Commissioner.

1928

1 February

Resignation of Damad Ahmad Nami and his Ministry after the new High Commissioner withdraws consent to the previous commitments to the nationalists of de Jouvenel.

10 February

Appointment of the Ministry of Sheikh Taj al-Din al-Husaini.

9 May

Meeting of the steering group which leads to the electoral victory of the National Bloc.

11 August

Voting by the Constituent Assembly on all 110 articles of the constitution. Among these are six articles that the French expect to be attached because they are not in harmony with Mandate rule. The High Commissioner, Ponsot, relies on the effect of this so he can annul the work of the Assembly.

1929

10 July

Opening of the amphitheatre building of the Syrian University.

4 November

Publication of Decree 1521, acknowledging the certificate of the Syrian baccalaureate as equivalent to the French baccalaureate.

28 December

Birth of the first daughter of Rida Saïd, Omayma.

1931

July

Farewell party for the Principal of the University, Dr Rida Saïd, on the occasion of his departure to Paris to represent Syria in the celebrations of the four-hundredth anniversary of the Collège de France.

16 November

Dismissal of the government of Sheikh Taj al-Din al-Husaini.

19 November

Setting up of a consultative council to implement the constitution under the chairmanship of Haqqi al-Azm with other members including Dr Rida Saïd. Their task is to prepare for elections to the Parliament that are to take place in December 1931.

1932

9 April

Results of the elections and appeal for the Parliament to be opened on 7 June. Muhammad Ali al-Abid is elected President of the Republic.

14 June

Formation of the first ministry of Haqqi al-Azm.

July

Dr Rida Saïd leaves his post as Dean of the Medical School to focus on his post as Principal of the Syrian University.

1933

12 October

Appointment of Count Damien de Martel as High Commissioner in place of Henri Ponsot.

1934

9 April

Foundation of the Surgical Society in Damascus and the appointment of Dr Rida Saïd as its President.

17 May

Resignation of the government of Haqqi al-Azm and the formation of a new government under Sheikh Taj al-Din al-Husaini.

1935

14 April

Birth of Rida Saïd's second daughter, Houzama.

17–22 June

Holding of the Eighth Conference of the Egyptian Medical Society in Damascus under the chairmanship of Dr Ali Pasha Ibrahim.

1936

22 February

Publication of Order no 139, in accordance with a request from Dr Rida Saïd, Principal of the Syrian University, placing him on the retirement list. He goes back to his work in his private clinic.

23 February

Resignation of the ministry of Sheikh Taj al-Din al-Husaini at the suggestion of the High Commissioner, de Martel, who sees him reaching an understanding with the Syrian Nationalists about having a treaty between France and Syria.

Formation of a neutral government under Ata al-Ayubi, to prepare this treaty and arrange to send a Syrian delegation to Paris to negotiate with the French government.

15 March

Syrian negotiating delegation leaves for Paris, led by Hashim al-Atasi.

7 September

Publication of Order no 756, appointing Professor Abdul Qadir al-Azm, Dean of the School of Law, as Principal of the Syrian University in place of Dr Rida Saïd.

9 September

Celebration of the signing of the Franco-Syrian Treaty at the French Ministry of Foreign Affairs.

Return of the Syrian delegation from Paris after the signing of the Franco-Syrian Treaty, and the holding of elections, won by the National Bloc. Election of Hashim al-Atasi as President of the Republic and the appointment of Jamal Mardam Bek as Prime Minister.

Agreement of the Treaty by the Syrian Parliament.

Obstruction to agreement of the Treaty in the French Parliament.

Demonstrations over the Treaty and the fate of the Province of Alexandretta/Iskenderun.

Appointment of Gabriel Puaux as High Commissioner in place of Count de Martel.

1938

28 April

Birth of Rida Saïd's third daughter, Racha.

1939

28 June

Detachment of the Province of Alexandretta/Iskenderun, from Syria in accordance with a Franco-Turkish agreement, and its annexation to Turkey.

July

Resignation of President Hashim al-Atasi.

Cancellation of work on the constitution and the dissolution of Parliament. National government terminated by High Commissioner Puaux.

Establishment of a government of administrators under Bahij al-Khatib.

1 September

Outbreak of the Second World War.

21 December

Birth of Rida Saïd's third son, Wafic.

1940

22 June

Collapse of France before the German advance and the signing of a truce with Germany that sets up a collaborationist government under Marshal Pétain in the city of Vichy. In response General de Gaulle establishes the Free French government first in London and then in Algiers.

The Vichy government appoints General Dentz as High Commissioner to replace Puaux, who joins de Gaulle in Algiers.

1941

8 June

French aircraft fly above Damascus, dropping leaflets coming from General Catroux, representative of Free France in the Levant. They announce, in the name of the leader, General de Gaulle, that Free France is coming to put an end to the Mandate over Syria and Lebanon, and proclaim their independence. Indeed Free French forces on 14 July arrive and clear out the forces belonging to the Vichy government.

Sheikh Taj al-Din al-Husaini is appointed to the Presidency of the Republic with Hasan al-Hakim as Prime Minister.

27 September

General Catroux, the Free French High Commissioner in the Levant, presents the Syrian government with a written announcement proclaiming Syria's independence.

1942

Arrival of the British General Edward Spears in Damascus.

1943

16 January

Death of the President of the Republic, Sheikh Taj al-Din al-Husaini.

Two governments follow that of Hasan al-Hakim. First is the government of Husni al-Barazi, and then that of Jamil al-Ulshi, whose rule is terminated by Catroux on 25 March. Understanding with the leaders of the National Bloc on holding elections under the auspices of the neutral government, led by Ata al-Ayubi. The National Bloc wins an overwhelming majority and the new Parliament elects Shukri al-Quwwatli as President of the Republic on 17 August.

Jean Helleu replaces Catroux as High Commissioner.

The Ministries of Sa'dallah al-Jabiri and then Faris al-Khuri.

23 December

Agreement between the French and Syrian governments on handing over joint interests in Syria and Lebanon to Syrians and Lebanese.

1945

26 February

Syria declares war on Germany and Japan.

22 March

Signing of the charter of the League of Arab States in Cairo.

31 March

Syria is invited to the San Francisco Conference that launches the United Nations Organisation.

May

Arrival in Damascus of Senegalese forces under the command of a French officer at a time when Syrians are expecting the departure of what is left of French forces.

8 May

High Commissioner General Beynet presents to the two governments of Syria and Lebanon a request they sign up to three points: the independence of French cultural institutions, the maintenance of French economic interests and the establishment of French air and naval bases in the two countries.

26 May

Session of the Syrian Parliament and unanimous rejection of the French requests.

29 May

French forces shell the Syrian Parliament and destroy the police station with great loss of life.

31 May

The British Army instructs the French forces to withdraw from Syria and says that Britain must take over the military command in their place with immediate effect. This is after British Prime Minister Winston Churchill sends a firmly worded telegram to General de Gaulle ordering his forces to return to their barracks.

26 August

Formation of a ministry under Faris al-Khuri, followed on 30 September by the ministry of Sa'dallah al-Jabiri.

28 October

Death of Dr Rida Saïd.

NOTES

1 The Awakening

1. This was the first Balkan War in which Bulgaria, Serbia, Montenegro and Greece fought together to get rid of Ottoman rule.
2. Yuzbashi, the Ottoman military rank that is equivalent to captain.
3. Effendi was a formal term of respect for an official of a certain rank. The English equivalent would be sir.
4. Bustan al-A'jam is the quarter of Damascus that is today al-Halbuni.
5. *Kul ağasi* is an Ottoman rank equivalent to major.

2 Formation

1. Ahmad Qadri worked on forming the management of the Young Arabs Society (al-Fatat) with Awni Abdul Hadi, Muhammad Rustum Haidar, Rafiq al-Tamimi, Sabri al-Khuja, Muhammad Mihmasani, Tawfiq al-Natur and Abdul Ghani al-Arisi.

2. Mar'i Pasha al-Mallah later became the representative for Aleppo in the Syrian Congress that was held in Damascus, 1919–20, and was elected as deputy to President Hashim al-Atasi.

3 The Giving

1. The Hijaz Station is the principal railway station in Damascus. It was built after the Hijaz Railway link to Madina was completed in 1908.
2. Muhajirin is the quarter of Jabal Qasiyun that towers over Damascus.
3. The term the Medical School (*madrasa*), as in the Arab Medical School, developed into the Arab Medical Faculty or College (*kulliya*). In 1920 it was given the name Arab Medical Institute/School (*ma'had*) until it became one of the faculties (*kulliya*) of the university after 1946, when it was called the Faculty of Medicine.
4. The committee for establishing the Arab Medical School was initially composed of Dr Ahmad Ratib al-Sabban, Tahir al-Jaza'iri, Hikmat al-Muradi, Sa'id al-Suyuti, Zakhur al-Abid (Director of Health in the Police) and the chemist Tawfiq Latuf. Some of these became the first members of the teaching staff of the Arab Medical School. But Dr Shahbandar withdrew from the committee and from the teaching staff afterwards to devote himself to political work. Dr Hamuda also resigned. He was given the task of organising health issues in the

Hijaz, and Dr al-Zahra resigned because of his work as head of the medical staff of the Arab Army.

5. The National Hospital was constructed in 1899 when Husain Nazim Pasha was Wali. At the time it had the name Mustashfa al-Ghuraba (Foreigners' Hospital), then in the Faisal years became the National Hospital.

6. The Turkish Medical School was first founded in Damascus in 1903. Its first temporary base was in the house of Ziwar Pasha al-Azm in Salihiya Road. This rented building included halls for instruction, laboratories for chemistry, physics, anatomy and physiology. In 1913 those in charge of managing it were able to construct a larger two-storey building in the garden of the Mustashfa al-Ghuraba (Foreigners' Hospital), later the National Hospital. The lower floor was allocated to the laboratories and the upper floor to the teaching of theory. After Turkey entered the First World War the Medical School was transferred to Beirut where it occupied buildings of the Jesuit Fathers who had left at the beginning of the war. The school remained in these buildings until the end of the war, when the Jesuit Fathers returned. That was more or less the end of the Turkish Medical School after its life in Damascus and Beirut for the fifteen years between 1903 and 1918. During that time 110 doctors graduated, as well as 152 pharmacists who received instruction in medicine and pharmacy through the medium of Turkish.

7. Among those who first undertook teaching at the Arab Medical School were the following doctors: Rida Saïd,

Sa'id al-Suyuti, Husam al-Din Abu'l-Sa'ud, Muhammad Sadiq al-Tarabishi, Murshid Khatir, Abdul Qadir Radi, Mahmud Hamdi Hamuda, Adib al-Ja'fari, Sami al-Sati, Ibrahim al-Sati, Jamil al-Khani, Michel Shamandi, Abdul Qadir Sirri, Mustafa Shawqi, Ahmad Ratib al-Sabban, Sa'id Shaikh al-Ard, Munif al-A'idi, Ilyas al-Murr, Tawfiq al-Daqar, Abdullah al-Tinawi, Ahmad Hamdi al-Khayyat, Abdul Rahman Shahbandar, Philip Barakat, Khairi al-Kabbani, Sidqi al-Malhas, Satraki Chan, Tahir al-Jaza'iri, Hasib Bayzid, Hamdi Amin, Kamil Hilal and Ali Rida al-Jundi, Among the chemists were Abdul Wahhab al-Qanawati, Fahmi Abu'l-Sa'ud, Shawkat al-Jarrah, Tawfiq Latuf and Munir al-Muha'iri. Many of them did not continue teaching and excused themselves from continuing because of their limited Arabic or for other reasons.

8. Niqula Ziada said when he was writing about the translation movement, "Translation started in the days of al-Mansur; it became stronger and better organised in the days of al-Rashid, al-Ma'mun and al-Mutawakkil. It first dealt with the practical sciences – medicine, astronomy, astrology ... then it included philosophy, logic, mathematics and physical engineering.

"During the *Jahiliya*, the period before the Prophet Muhammad, Arabs were aware of winds and hurricanes, gave names to the stars, and knew about the orbit of the sun and moon. But less than two centuries after the death of the Prophet the Arabic language extended to include astronomical concepts. It also extended to medicine, natural history and engineering. The Arabs did not give up translating but wrote on all modern subjects and this is still important in issues of translation. The language needed new expressions and constructs for new tasks, The Arabic language responded to all these challenges. The linguistic vessel that had earlier not known something, expanded its capacity so that it included every kind of knowledge and science. The tool that had expressed a limited amount of ideas and thoughts was able afterwards to express all that was new. If the Arabic language did not find within its lexicon something that gave new meaning it coined it from Arabic and made it contemporary and gave it an Arab stamp. It did not refuse a new idea because appropriate words were outside the Arabic lexicon. New intellectual life necessitated a new style in writing. Arabic went along with this and developed its own style, introducing various images and expressions for new things.

"The new thoughts called for a style of writing that had depth, width, fluidity, dynamism and logic to express these needs. Similarly it demanded that the language provide the necessary words. When al-Razi wrote on medicine he could only resort to what he investigated and linked what he wanted to what he intended.

"Arabic was able to deal with all this and to make it easy to provide every writer with what he needed in vocabulary and technical terms. This proves that Arabic at any age is the product of the genius of its people. For if the nation has ideas and knowledge and dynamism then its language can fit in with those ideas, knowledge and dynamism. If the nation is turned in on itself then the language is similarly turned in on itself; the language is like the people."

9. The American doctors who taught medicine in the American University of Beirut were Van Dyck, who spent twenty-five years perfecting his Arabic language with the teacher Butrus al-Bustani, and his colleagues Post, Wortabet and Lewis. They wrote twelve medical books in Arabic, published in Beirut between 1869 and 1882.

10. The most prominent opponent of the teaching of medicine in Arabic was Muhammad Kurd Ali, head of the Arabic Scientific Academy, on the grounds that he feared that the language would be corrupted by people who did not know its principles and were not fluent in it.

11. This was the famous calligrapher Mamduh al-Sharif (1886–1934), the sheikh of the Damascus calligraphers who was outstanding in the *thulth* style of writing. Many of the great Syrian calligraphers studied under him, such as Badri al-Dirani and Hilmi al-Habbab.

12. The first batch of graduates at the Arab Medical College were made up of the final-year students of the Medical School in Beirut who had studied medicine through the medium of Turkish. When they came to Damascus after the war the Dean of the Medical School, Dr Rida Saïd,

arranged a special course for them so they could complete their medical studies and then sit for an examination in Arabic. They all passed and were entitled to diplomas in medicine. Among them were three Lebanese – Jamal Haji Yusuf, Ali al-Ghandur and Walim Na'ima. There was one Iraqi, Abdullah Istifan, and one Egyptian, Ali al-Husri. The rest were Syrian: Yahya al-Shamma', Jawdat al-Kayyal, Mahmud al-Ra'is, Ahmad Yasin al-Ojjeh, Kamal Ashrafiya, Fuad Qadah, Zaki al-Shamma', Husni Sabah, Wahid Haqqi, Fahmi al-Hamawi, Ali al-Lahham, Zaki al-War', Sharif al-Rifa'i, Zaki al-Fahham, Ismail al-Usta, Sa'dallah Kamil, Sa'id Musa Pasha, Ahmad Shafiq Nasri, Muhi al-Din al-Quwwatli, Riyad al-Safadi, Wifa'i al-Bunni, Bahjat al-Atasi, Muhammad Qasim Agha, Sa'd al-Rajula, Taisir al-Khani, Abdul Hamid Shafaqa, Abdul Ghani Shahbandar, Mukhtar al-Mufti, Mustafa al-Kayy-ali, Muhammad Dular, Kamal al-Husni, Dia al-Barudi, Rida al-Attar, Abdul Razzaq al-Saqqa', Muhammad Khair al-Sab', Ala' al-Din al-Salti, Fathi Fawq al-'Ada, Muham-mad al-Husami, Tawfiq al-Dibasi, Subhi al-Katib, Jamil al-Sharabi, Mustafa al-Mawlawi and Mustafa al-Ma'ashli.

13. The Arab Medical School opened on 12 January 1919, and Dr Rida Saïd was appointed Dean. The School of Law opened on 25 September the same year, and at the start Professor Abdul Latif Salah was appointed Dean; he was then succeeded by Professor Abdul Qadir al-Azm.

14. Shakir al-Hanbali (1876–1958) was among the first to work in the public sector. After finishing his higher

studies at the Malkiya School in Istanbul he held a number of important administrative posts during the Ottoman period, such as provincial governor of Hama and then of Acre. After Syria became independent during the Faisal period, he was head of general communications with the Military Governor, General Rida al-Rikabi. During the Mandate era he was elected member of the representative assembly in 1923 and was chosen to be its Speaker. In 1926 he became Minister of Education and then Minister of Justice. During his time as Minister of Education he issued the decree making elementary education compulsory. After the opening of the School of Law in 1919 he worked there as a professor and taught administrative law, basic law and law relating to land and religious endowments (*waqfs*). He was a pioneer journalist, having published the first Arab newspaper in Istanbul – *al-Hadara* ("Civilisation"), jointly with Abdul Hamid al-Zahrawi. During the Mandate years he published the newspaper *al-Qalam* ("The Pen") in Damascus, but the Mandate authorities closed it down. In the Faisal period he was given the task of founding the newspaper *al-Asima* and of being its Editor-in-Chief. It was later known as *al-Jarida al-Rasmiya* ("The Official Gazette").

15. Professor Shakir al-Hanbali of the College of Law recalls that "in May 1929 I came to Damascus at the same time as two groups – of George Abyad, and Yusuf Wahbi (known as Ramses) – came together to put on a joint production. The Syrian government gave them a very warm

welcome. The Prime Minister attended the first night of the play 'Confession Chair'. As was his custom Dr Rida Saïd hosted a great reception in the Khawwam Hotel on behalf of the university in appreciation of the initiatives of the two groups in giving free tickets to all the university staff and students. The reception that took place on Monday 13 May in honour of the actors turned into a literary celebration during which there were speeches given by Yusuf Wahbi, George Abyad and Ma'ruf al-Arna'ut, and the Lebanese poet Amin Nakhla (a student in the third year in the School of Law in Damascus) who recited a poem of warm welcome.

"There was a group of university professors near me at that reception. Among them I remember Dr Abdul Qadir al-Azm, Dean of the School of Law, Dr Fa'iz al-Khuri, who delivered a beautiful speech on behalf of the university, Dr Munif al-A'idi, Dr Tahir al-Jaza'iri, Dr Mustafa Shawqi and Dr Abdul Qadir Sirri as well as a good number of other staff and students. There was delightful conversation around the table between Dr Rida Saïd and Yusuf Wahbi and George Abyad which made me realise that the Principal of the university had a profound and extensive knowledge of world theatre. During his medical studies in Paris he made a point of seeing the best theatre, especially performances of the famous French actor Lucien Guitry, under whom George Abyad had been a student. We also learned for the first time that Dr Rida Saïd had plans for adding to the existing faculties a Faculty for Fine Art to teach drawing, sculpture, drama and music. This shows that this remarkable man had a clear vision for the future, and that his one idea was to enlarge the university and extend its range of learning so that it would rank among the universities of the advanced countries."

The Damascus newspaper *al-Qabas* ("The Firebrand") in its 14 May 1929 edition had a detailed description of the university party for the great actors and reported the speeches made there. Among the remarks made by George Abyad were that he was a son of Bilad al-Sham and that he felt at home in Damascus. And Yusuf Wahbi indicated that he had called that morning on Tawfiq al-Kabbani, grandson of the pioneer of Arab musical theatre Ahmad Abu Khalil al-Kabbani who brought this new art form to Egypt. He added that his visit was to pay homage to this immortal Syrian artist. Then Professor Fa'iz al-Khuri, who taught in the Faculty of Law, said in his speech, "If Egypt has given to the Arabs this genius of the theatre Yusuf Wahbi, who has promoted this art form and saved it from corruption, Damascus has already given another Yusuf to Egypt, and that is Yusuf al-Sadiq, God bless him, who has saved it from famine."

16. On 31 August 1920 General Gouraud issued an edict creating Greater Lebanon. It became operative from 1 September.

17. Maysalun: a site on the Beirut–Damascus road where on 24 July 1920 a battle took place between a huge French

force advancing to occupy Damascus and the Arab Army, under the command of the Minister of Defence, General Yusuf al-Azma, attempting to check this advance. The battle lasted only four hours. The Arab forces were defeated because of the disparity in numbers of men and effectiveness of weapons. The Minister al-Azma died a heroic martyr's death on the field of battle. After this the French were able to complete their march on Damascus under the command of General Goybet. Damascus was occupied the following day.

18. The two occasions when Prince Faisal went to Europe were on 22 November 1918 and 13 September 1919.

19. His third ministry was formed, the last of the Faisal era, on 26 July 1920, under Ala' al-Din al-Durubi. Its membership included Abdul Rahman al-Yusuf. Both were assassinated later, on 31 August, when they tried to calm things down in the Hauran. The other members were Ata al-Ayubi, Badi' al-Mu'ayyad, Jalal Zuhdi, Faris al-Khuri, Jamil al-Ulshi and Yusuf al-Hakim.

20. Yusuf al-Hakim (1879–1979) was born in Lattakia and was outstanding in law, administration and politics. He was chosen as Vice-Chairman of the Syrian Congress in 1919 and became a minister three times during the Faisal years, and three times during the Mandate. He was the President of the Court of Cassation until 1948.

21. Abdul Qadir al-Azm (1884–1964) was among the most prominent of those who held important posts at various times in Syria. After completing his higher studies in

Istanbul he was appointed district officer, *qa'immaqam*, in a number of administrative districts in both Greater Syria and in the Ottoman European provinces. In the Faisal era he was named Director of Publications. Under the Mandate he was Dean of the School of Law where he also used to teach economics. He was Minister of Finance in the second ministry of Damad Ahmad Nami in 1926. After the retirement of Dr Rida Saïd in 1936 he followed him as Principal of the Syrian University. In 1941 he was appointed Chairman of the Consultative Council. Then between 1944 and 1949 he became the agent of the Syrian government with the Syrian Company for the Tobacco Monopoly. He was known, throughout his public life, for his independent mind and objectivity, his impartiality and his courage in confronting wrongdoing. Among the most outstanding of the stands he took in his young manhood in Istanbul was sending angry letters replying to the press campaign conducted by the Turkish racists attacking Arabs.

22. In chapter 7 of General Georges Catroux's memoirs that had the title *Deux Missions en Moyen-Orient 1919–1922*, he says he indeed wrote to General Gouraud to dissuade him from the idea of closing the Schools of Medicine and Law in Damascus. In his answering minute he employed the arguments made by Dr Rida Saïd but without mentioning his name. As a result of this the idea of closing the two Damascus schools was put to one side. He was not influenced by the grudge of Father Chanteur,

Superior of St Joseph's Jesuit University, who showed hostility to Catroux and launched anathemas against him for many years. Catroux returned to Beirut in 1941 on a new mission. By this time he had become a general and commander of the forces of the Levant and Permanent Delegate and representative of the leader of the Free French in the Levantine States. On 27 November 1941 he announced the independence of Syria. When he came back to Beirut Father Chanteur was still sending hostile cables about him. But Catroux discovered that he was also a supporter of Marshal Pétain and the Vichy government. He was still being woundingly critical of Catroux and of the commander of the Free French, General De Gaulle. In the end Catroux was obliged to have him transferred to a Jesuit monastery in Egypt where he spent the rest of his life. (See pp. 56–67 of Catroux's memoirs.)

23. Henri de Jouvenel: A member of the French Senate, he was descended from an aristocratic family. For a while he was the Editor-in-Chief of the newspaper *Le Matin*. He married the famous novelist Colette and was Minister of Education.

He was the first civilian High Commissioner after three generals. As soon as he arrived at his place of work on 2 December 1925, he stretched his hand out to Syrian nationals and agreed to their demands, such as a general pardon for political prisoners who had been arrested by the previous High Commissioner, General Sarrail, the acceptance of Syria in the League of Nations, the call for elections to the Constitutional Assembly, negotiations towards a Syrian–French Treaty to take the place of the French Mandate, founding a national army and achieving Syrian unity. These issues, and especially the issue of the treaty, were an acknowledgement that Syria was an independent state. The French government let de Jouvenel down and did not agree to his policy, and so he resigned from his post in June 1926, that is, just six months after his appointment.

24. Dr Murshid Khatir (1888–1961) was one of the first doctors on the teaching staff of the Arab Medical School, being there from its foundation in 1919 until his retirement in 1958 as Professor of Surgery. He became Dean of the Faculty of Medicine in 1947 and Minister of Health in 1952. In 1953 he was elected Chairman of the sixth session of the World Health Organisation in Geneva. He was an outstanding pioneer of medical writing in Arabic, and coined thousands of new medical terms. He published numerous books and articles and medical reference works under his own name or in cooperation with colleagues. He was at the forefront of those doctors who conscientiously elevated the Arabic language of medicine, casting it in a form that was elegant and precise. He was elected a member of a number of scientific bodies, including the Arab Scientific Academy of Damascus, the French Scientific Academy in Paris and the Military Medical Academy of Brazil. He received a large number of Arab and foreign awards.

25. The *Journal of the Arab Medical School* continued to be published every month until April 1947.

26. Dr Izzat Muraidan graduated from the Arab Medical School in 1930. During his studies he was always among the most distinguished. He was the first to win the competition to be selected to work in the National Hospital. He came first in the competition to be Assistant Professor for Anatomy in the Medical School. In 1935 he was sent to Paris for three years to follow his specialism. When he returned to Damascus he was appointed Assistant Professor in the Department of Surgery and it was not long before he became head of this department, then full Professor of Medicine and Therapy. In 1956 he was elected Dean of the Faculty of Medicine, and stayed in this post until 1964. Dr Muraidan published an important collection of articles on medicine and on the subject of therapy, and one book, *Studies and Speculations in Science, Medicine and Life*. It included a number of lectures he gave in Damascus and in other Arab capitals.

27. Elections for the Representative Assembly were held while Haqqi al-Azm was Governor of Damascus. It was made up of thirty members: Ata al-Ajlani (Damascus), Abdul Hamid Qaltaqji (Damascus), Abu'l Khair al-Jundi (Homs), Abdul Qadir al-Kaylani (Hama), Rashid al-Barazi (Hama), Anis al-Suriani (Homs), Shakir al-Qayim (Damascus), Muhammad Khairi Aqil (al-Nabk), As'ad al-Naqari (Homs), Shakir al-Hanbali (Damascus), Habib Kahhali (Damascus), Ahmad al-Fayyad

(Qariatain and Jubb al-Jarrah), Faidi al-Atasi (Homs), Faris al-Zu'bi (Izra'), Tamir Mustafa (al-Salimiya), Badi' al-Mu'ayyad (Damascus), Mahmud al-Jijakli (Hama), Abdul Nabi al-Jarudi (Jarud), Sami Pasha Mardam Bey (Damascus), Abdul Hamid al-Attar (Damascus), Ali al-Khatib (Wadi al-Ajam), Husain al-Ibsh (Damascus), Najm al-Din al-Durubi (Homs), Muhammad Sa'id Ramadan (al-Zabadani), Ahmad al-Yusuf (Damascus), Sa'di al-Jijakli (Duma), Arslan Ali (al-Qantara), Rushdi al-Sukkari (Damascus), Ahmad Jum'a al-Hariri (Izra') and Sa'd al-Din al-Mikdad (Dar'a).

28. The magazine *al-Asima* published the following in its issue 211 of 22 August 1921 amendment.

"We have received a letter from the respected Principal of the Medical School that was sent to our magazine: 'We have read in some of the local press a paragraph with the title "Chemical Analysis" in which appears the words "The Directorate of Public Justice has, based on a letter from the Directorate of Public Health, published that henceforth the substances required for analysis are to be sent to the chemical laboratory at the Directorate of Public Health and not to the laboratory of the Medical School. This is because the laboratory at the Medical School does not meet the conditions that qualify it to conduct these analyses etc." We have sought an explanation from the Directorate of Public Health of the meaning of the words "does not meet the conditions" that were directed at our school which is in possession of every technical facility.' The Directorate replied that the meaning was that it was working according to a law that had recently been issued relating to forensic medicine. Matters of medical examinations touching legal issues came within the exclusive jurisdiction of the doctors of the legal department. Analyses relating in this way are required to be conducted in the chemical laboratory belonging to the Directorate of Public Health. This phrase was not directed at the competence of the Medical School, or to state that they had insufficient equipment for this purpose. The determining factor was to lighten the many burdens of the aforesaid laboratory that deals with teaching."

29. Lutfi al-Haffar, one of the great men of Syria, distinguished for his political, economic and social work. He became a minister several times, then Prime Minister in 1939. His name was linked to the pioneering project of bringing the pure waters of Ain al-Fijja to the residences of Damascus and working on it for ten years; it was inaugurated in 1932.

30. Shukri al-Quwwatli, the great Syrian political figure whose name is associated with the national struggle for independence. He became President of the Republic on 17 August 1943.

31. General Maxime Weygand, the High Commissioner who replaced Gouraud on 9 May 1923.

32. In his memoirs Professor Lutfi al-Haffar mentions that he was very keen that Dr Rida Saïd would be present

at every meeting of the board. He expressed his delight when he returned to attend the board meetings after a prolonged absence because of being very busy with the examinations at the Medical School or when he had been sent on academic missions abroad. Professor al-Haffar said about him, "He was among the members who knew what they were doing."

33. The order establishing the Syrian University was issued on 15 June 1923 during the government of Subhi Barakat, President of the State of Syria. It had the approval of the French High Commissioner, General Maxime Weygand. At its foundation the university consisted of the School of Law and the School of Medicine, the Arab Medical Academy and the Damascus Museum. On 15 March 1926 Order number 238 was issued separating the academy and the museum from the university. This was while Damad Ahmad Nami was President.

34. The Council of the Syrian University was made up of Dr Rida Saïd, Chairman, and, as members, Dr Abdul Qadir al-Azm, Dean of the School of Law, doctors and professors in the School of Medicine Murshid Khatir, Munif al-A'idi and Mustafa Shawqi, and, from the School of Law, Shakir al-Hanbali, Uthman Sultan and Sami Midani.

35. In the speech delivered by the Dean of the School of Law Professor Abdul Qadir al-Azm at a ceremony to see Dr Rida Saïd off on one of his academic missions abroad, he said, "I am not exaggerating when I say that Dr Rida Saïd is a genius in every sense of the word. The university is

dependent on Dr Rida Saïd" (see Part 6, Volume 2, p. 371
of the *Journal of the Arab Medical School*).

36. Faris al-Khuri, 1877–1962, was one of the leading lights
of politics, culture and law, as well as the national struggle in Syria. He held ministerial posts and was Prime
Minister and Speaker of the House of Representatives
more than once. He was Professor in the School of Law
in Damascus, and a member of the Syrian delegation that
negotiated the Franco-Syrian Treaty in Paris in 1936. In
the mid-1940s he became one of the most prominent
representatives at the United Nations where he defended
Syrian independence, spoke on the Egyptian problem
and the Palestine issue. He was Chairman of the Security
Council twice, in 1947 and 1948.

37. Ata al-Ayubi, 1874–1950, a well-known statesman who
held the posts of Minister and Prime Minister more than
once, starting from the Faisal period. At the end of the
Mandate period he was Head of State forming a non-
aligned ministry to carry out legislative elections which
resulted in a victory for the National Bloc.

38. After the Syrian state was established resulting from the
union of the statelets of Aleppo and Damascus, a ministry was formed on 20 December 1924 made up of Ata
al-Ayubi, Minister of Justice, Nasri Bakhash, Minister
of the Interior, Jalal Zuhdi, Minister of Finance, Rida
Saïd, Minister of Education and Hasan Izzat, Minister
of Public Works, Agriculture and the Economy. It lasted
until February 1926.

39. The Ghouta is a collection of orchards surrounding the city of Damascus, irrigated by the Barada River.

40. The Bani Yas is one of seven tributaries of the Barada River.

41. The Yazid is another of the seven tributaries of the Barada River.

42. Madame Adila Baihum al-Jaza'iri, 1900–75, was a distinguished pioneer in the field of Syrian female emancipation. She played an outstanding role in founding women's societies, and educational, charitable and social organisations, in activities supporting the national struggle and in issues of freedom in different parts of the Arab world.

43. Philippe Berthelot had been an extremist working on the expansion of French imperial influence to include Syria and Lebanon. He was an effective member of the colonialist party in what was called the Committee for French Asia that also included in the Ministry for Foreign Affairs François Georges Picot, who had drafted and signed the famous Sykes-Picot Treaty in 1916. This committed Britain and France to dividing their spheres of influence in the Ottoman provinces east of the Mediterranean after the war.

44. The collection of Syrian medical writings that were presented to the International Conference for Tropical Diseases in Cairo included:

    Diseases of the Eye for Practitioners, translated by Professor Rida Saïd.

Descriptive Anatomy by Abdul Qadir Sirri

The Science of Instincts by Munif al-A'idi

On Bacteria by Ahmad Hamdi al-Khayyat

Surgery and Therapy by Professor Trabaud, translated
by Murshid Khatir and Shawkat al-Shatti

The Science of Sutures by Professor Shawkat al-Shatti

A Treatise on Gynaecology by Professor Lecercle,
translated by Dr Murshid Khatir and Dr Shawkat
al-Shatti

Inorganic Chemistry by Professor Abdul Wahhab
al-Qanawati

Parasitology by Ahmad Hamdi al-Khayyat

Surgery of the Digestive Tubes by Professor Lecercle,
translated by Professor Murshid Khatir

Urology by Professor Lecercle, translated by Professor
Murshid Khatir

Chemical Studies by the pharmacist Salah al-Din
Mas'ud al-Kawakabi

Materials by Professor Abdul Wahhab al-Qanawati

Morbid Anatomy by Shawkat al-Shatti

45. Dr Ahmad Munif al-A'idi, 1886–1962, graduated from
the Medical School in Istanbul in 1906. On returning
to Damascus he opened a clinic for internal diseases and
paediatrics. He was in the forefront of the distinguished
group of doctors who founded the Arab Medical School
in 1919, and taught physiology there. Dr A'idi was among
the first to found private schools in Damascus. In 1907
he founded the National Scientific College in 1907. He

selected the cream of the best professors and teachers. The college was distinguished for graduating over the course of fifty years scores of people who became celebrated ministers, judges, doctors, pharmacists, lawyers, diplomats, industrialists, engineers, businessmen and senior civil servants. Dr Ahmad Munif al-A'idi became Dean of the Faculty of Medicine twice, in 1934 and 1947.

46. The construction of the auditorium of the Syrian University was completed six years after the building was equipped and officially opened on 10 July 1929. The Egyptian Medical Conference was the first important conference held there.

47. Dr Husni Sabah, 1900–86, was one of the first graduates of the Syrian Medical School – in the batch of 1919–20 – and obtained his doctorate in medicine from the University of Lausanne in Switzerland in 1925. He became Professor of Internal Diseases and their Treatment at the Arab Medical School in 1932 and was elected Dean of the Medical School in 1938 and appointed Principal of the Syrian University in 1943.

48. Dr Adnan Rida Saïd graduated from the Arab Medical School in 1939, and worked for a time in his father's clinic, then in his own private clinic, first in Deir ez-Zor and then in Damascus. In 1946 he was appointed Assistant Professor in Ophthalmology in the Faculty of Medicine. He was sent to France to study for a year, and then became head of the Ophthalmology Department in the Military Hospital at al-Mezze. In 1961 he became

head of the Ophthalmology Department in the Faculty
of Medicine in the University of Damascus, and head
of the Department of Head Diseases at the Charitable Hospital. He also had his clinic and wrote medical
books. In 1965, with a number of colleagues he founded
the Syrian Ophthalmology Society, of which he soon
became Chairman. In appreciation of his services he was
awarded the Order of Syrian Achievement, and it was
decided, on his retirement in 1973, to give his name to
one of the wings of the Faculty of Medicine.

49. Sura al-Baqara, verse 216. (Pickthall's translation.)

50. Dr Adnan Rida Saïd has written, "Most of the benefit
I obtained from working with my father in his clinic at
his side was in outstanding practical experience in medicine. Since 1920 he had been systematic in recording
data about patients who came to him for treatment. I
do not think any doctor of his generation had a similar
methodical system. He used to open up a register that
contained the name of the patient, his age, the date of
the consultation, the serial number in the sequence of
the patients who had visited the clinic, and all the information relating to the complaint, the date of the illness,
what diseases his parents and members of the family had
had, the medicines he was taking. After an examination
my father would record his observations, what he had
diagnosed, the medicine he prescribed, and the method
of treatment he was considering. He took care to write
this information in French, maintaining confidentiality

and intimacy in accordance with professional medical ethics and good practice. The book would be away from the eyes of the nurses in the clinic or of other curious patients who might come in when he was away from the clinic. When he wrote out the prescription he noted on it the serial number he had given in his register of patients. This was to ensure the correct drugs from the pharmacy that the patient would go to.

"My father, knowing the limited awareness of health matters among many people in those days, always tried to protect his patients from confusion or chance over the medicine he prescribed. I remember once he received a letter from Baghdad written by a patient whom he had treated fifteen months earlier. In his letter the man pointed out that he had not used the medicine that had been prescribed by my father and that he had lost the prescription. He was therefore asking for another new one which he should send to his address in Baghdad. My father replied very courteously, firmly and clearly, that he was unable to prescribe any medicine without examining him again to ascertain the course of the illness after that long time, so he could issue a prescription that was appropriate to his fresh state. He invited him to call in at the clinic when circumstances allowed him to come to Damascus.

"As for his humane dealings with needy patients, I do not know that he turned down a request that came to him from one of his colleagues or acquaintances to carry out an operation free of charge on one of those very poor people."

51. Dr Adnan Rida Saïd writes, "What pained my father most was the way those charlatans treated the eyes of the rural poor. They submitted them to practices that were harmful and painful and mutilated them; of no use at all. For example, cauterising the eyelids, or applying tar on them for many months or years. The eyelids were unable to move. Or branding the skin around the eyes with a lighted cigarette or with a piece of heated iron. These left injuries that were devastating, permanently oozing pus. He was also alarmed by what that band of charlatan women, known as *fashshashat*, did in the Euphrates valley. When someone from a rural area came to them complaining of a bloodshot eye, the fashshasha would roll her filthy tongue between the eyelids and the eyeball and then claim that she had extracted some mud or a piece of grass, a piece of wool or a pebble, or even a piece of wire that she had actually concealed in her mouth. The following day the patient would note that the inflammation had increased, that his eyelids had swollen and that one of them was stuck to the other. The next day he suffered from severe complicated conjunctivitis that might result in corneal ulceration or partial or total blindness. The amazing thing was that the fashshasha did not just treat human beings in this harmful manner, but was also employed in 'treating' the eyes of sheep and cattle; as a consequence she transferred the microbes on her tongue

from the eyes of these animals to the eyes of the poor country folk.

"He had an aversion to the imposters who 'treated' with spells on children by reciting charms and with amulets, and by dosing the patient with incense claiming that they were thereby expelling the evil spirits that had filled the child with envy and sorcery, and that their eyes after this "treatment" would go back to normal. Similarly the materials that all these charlatans did not hesitate to apply to the ruined eyes of these country folk were abominable and filthy. These include crushed hedgehog gall bladder, urine, bat's blood and goat dung.

"I saw dozens of these country people come to my father's clinic seeking his help. It may be he could make amends for the harm and disease those imposters had done to their eyes. My own observations of these victims were mostly from Deir ez-Zor. They came frequently to the clinic; this was another motive for my intention of going to the Euphrates valley. This was in line with a scheme my father had, to increase the number of doctors to be sent to the rural areas of Syria with the aim of curbing the harm inflicted on the people by these ignorant charlatans."

52. Surat Ta Ha, verse 114. (Pickthall's translation.)
53. The statistical reports of the Syrian University show that the students of the Schools of Medicine and Law in the first year were not more than the number of fingers on two hands. In the year in which Dr Rida Saïd retired, 1936, there were 1128 graduates, men and women, in the two schools.

BIBLIOGRAPHY

In Arabic

Ali Sultan, *Tarikh Suriya 1908–1918, Nihayat al-Hukm al-Turki*, Dar Tlass, Damascus, 1987

Ali Sultan, *Tarikh Suriya 1918–1920 Hukm Faisal bin al-Husain*, Dar Tlas, Damascus, 1969

Abdul Aziz Muhammad Awad, *al-Idara al-Uthmaniya fi Wilaya Suriya 1864–1914*, Dar al-Ma'arif bi Misr, Cairo, 1969

Sa'id Ahmad Barajawi, *al-Imbiraturiya al-Uthmaniya Tarikhha al-Siyasi wa'l-Askari*, al-Ahliya li'l-Nashr wa'l-Tawzi', 1980

Ali Hasun, *Tarikh al-Dawla al-Uthmaniya*, al-Maktab al-Islami, 1980

Tawfiq Ali Biru, *al-Arab wa'l-Turk fi'l-Ahd al-Dusturi al-Uthmani 1908–1916* (MA thesis), Institute for Higher Arab Studies, University of the Arab States, Cairo, 1960

Abdul Karim Rafiq, *al-Arab wa'l-Uthmaniyun*, Maktab Atlas, Damascus, 1974

Sati' al-Husri and Ahmad Qadri, *Yawm Maysalun, Mudhakkarat an al-Thawra al-Arabiya al-Kubra*, Maktab al-Kashshaf, Beirut, 1945; Matba'a Zaidun, Damascus, 1954

Yusuf al-Hakim, *Suriya wa'-Ahd al-Uthmani*, Dar al-Nahar, Beirut, 1966

Yusuf al-Hakim, *Suriya wa'l-Ahd al-Faisali*, Dar al-Nahar, Beirut, 1966

Yusuf al-Hakim, *Suriya wa'l-intidab al-Faransi*, Dar al-Nahar, Beirut, 1983

Fakhri al-Barudi, *Mudhakkarat al-Barudi*, al-Hayat, Beirut, 1951

Akram Hasan al-Ulabi, *al-Takwim (Hijri/Miladi)*, Dar al-Masadir, Beirut, 1962

Nadir al-Attar, *Tarikh Suriya fi'l-Usur al-Haditha, al-Juz' al-Awwal, 1908–1916*, al-Insha', 1962

Abdul Nafi' Shahin, *al-Khutut al-Hadidiya*, University of Damascus, 1986

Muhammad Sa'id al-Ustuwani, *Mashahid wa Ahdath Dimashqiya*, Dar al-Jumhuriya

Yusuf Na'isa, *Mujtama' Madina Dimashq fi'l-Qarn al-Tasi' Ashr*, Dar Tlass, Damascus, 1986

Qaniba Shihabi, *Dimashq, Tarikh wa Suwar*, Ministry of Culture, Damascus, 1986

Khalid al-Azm, *Mudhakkarat, al-Juz' al-Awwal*, al-Dar al-Muttahida li'l-Nashr, Beirut, 1973

Izzat Muraidan, *al-Ustadh al-Duktur Ahmad Munif Uthman al-A'idi*, Matabi' al-Adib, Damascus, 1996

Shawkat al-Shatti, *Tarikh al-Tibb (Kitab al-Tibb fi Suriya min Bilad al-Sham)*, University of Damascus, 1960

Najib al-Armanazi, *Suriya min al-Ihtilal hatta al-Jala'*, Dar
al-Kitab al-Jadid, Beirut, 1973

Abdul Qadir al-Azm, *al-Mudhakkarat*, Matba'a al-Thabat,
Damascus, 1962

Salma al-Haffar al-Kuzbari, *Lutfi al-Haffar,
Mudhakkaratuhu, Hayatu wa Asru*, Riyad al-Rayis,
Beirut, 1997

Samir Antaki, *Rawwad Tibb al-Uyun fi Suriya*, Dar
al-Dhakira, Homs, 1993

Niqula Ziada, *Arabiyyat*, Riyad al-Rayis, Beirut, 1994

Husni Subh and Bashir al-Azma, *Mujiz an al-Amrad
al-Batina*, Syrian University, Damascus, 1946

Akmal Kamal al-Din Ihsan Ughli, *Istanbul, Itlala ala'l-
Madi* (in Arabic, Turkish and English), Research Centre
for History, Arts and Islamic Culture, Istanbul, 1992

Zuhair Naji, *Tatawwur al-Tarbiya fi Suriya mundhu Matla'
al-Qarn al- Tasi' 'ashr hatta 1970*, unpublished MA thesis,
1977

Abdul Salam al-Ujaili, *Iyada fi'l-Rif*, Dar al-Sharq al-Arabi,
Beirut, 1977

Nasuh Babil, *al-Watha'iq wa'l-Mu'ahadat fi Bilad al-Arab*,
Al-Ayyam newspaper, no date

Salma Mardam Bek, *Awraq Jamil Mardam Bek (Istiqlal
Suriya)*, Sharikat Matbu'at li'l-Tawzi' wa'l-Nashr, Beirut,
1994

Hanna Khabbaz and Jurj Haddad, *Faris al-Khuri Hayatu
wa Asru*, Matabi' Sadir Rihani, Beirut, 1953

In English

Andrew Wheatcroft, *The Ottomans, Dissolving Images*,
Penguin Books, London, 1993

David Fromkin, *A Peace to End all Peace*, Avon Books, New
York, 1990

Philip S Khoury, *Urban Notables and Arab Nationalism*,
University Press, Cambridge, 1983

Philip S Khoury, *Syria and the French Mandate*, I B Tauris,
London, 1987

Patrick Kinross, *Ataturk*, Phoenix, London, 1995

Irfan Orga, *Portrait of a Turkish Family*, Eland, London,
1993

Michael Raeburn (ed), *Renoir*, Harry N Abrams Inc, New
York, 1985

Eliezer Tauber, *The Formation of Modern Syria and Iraq*,
Frank Cass, London, 1995

Stephen H Longrigg, *Syria and Lebanon under French
Mandate*, Royal Institute for International Affairs,
Librairie du Liban, Beirut, 1968

In French

Pierre Renouvin, *La Crise Européenne 1904–1914*, Felix
Alcan, Paris, 1996

Pierre Fournié and Jean-Louis Riccioli, *La France et Le
Proche-Orient*, Casterman, Paris, 1996

Klaus-Jürgen Sembach, *L'Art Nouveau*, Taschen, Cologne,
1993

Anne Bonny, *Les Années 10* (2 volumes), Editions du
  Regard, Paris, 1991
Jean-Claude Berchet, *Le Voyage en Orient*, Robert Laffort,
  Paris, 1985
Généau Moyen-ral Catroux, *Deux Missions au Moyen-
  Orient (1919–1922)*, Paris, 1985
Gabriel Puaux, *Deuz Années au Levant: Souvenirs de Syrie
  at du Liban*, Hachette, Paris, 1952

In Armenian

Toros Turanian, *History of the Baron Hotel Aleppo*, Sirkis
  Abdalian, Beirut, 1987

Miscellaneous Papers, Documents and Periodicals

The book, *Ahwal al-Ma'muriyin* (working log of Dr Rida
  Siad), kept between 1902 and 1928. Government of the
  Syrian State.
Pictures and Papers. Taken from the Centre for Research in
  Islamic History, Arts and Culture, Istanbul.
Pictures and Papers. Taken from Cerrah Pasha Hospital,
  Department of the History of Turkish Medicine,
  Istanbul.
The lecture of Dr Izzat Muraidan on Dr Rida Saïd. Arab
  Medical Conference, 1945.
Annual Reports of the Syrian University, 1928–29, 1930–31.
  Ministry of Education, Damascus, 1929, 1931.

Booklets of Ain al-Fijja Water Authority, Damascus.
Statement and Explanation of the Board for the Ain
al-Fijja Water Authority.
Prospectus for the concession of the project of Ain al-Fijja
and its follow-up. Supplement to Number 263 of the
magazine, *al-Asima*, the official magazine of the Syrian
Republic, Damascus, February 1924.
Prospectus regarding the distribution of water from Ain
al-Fijja to the city of Damascus. Board for the Ain al-Fijja
Water Authority, 1932.
Numbers of the *Journal of the Arab Medical School*, from
January 1924 to April 1947.
From *Hamm fi'l-Alam al-Arabi*, Part 1. Library for Arab and
Syrian Studies, Damascus, 1957.
Twenty Sixth Annual Report, Al-Sharq Hospital, Beirut,
1973.
Numbers of the newspaper, *al-Muqtabas*. Damascus, 1925.
Numbers of the newspaper, *al-Qabas*. Damascus, 1929.
Minutes of meetings of the Board of the Ain al-Fijja Water
Authority. From 1924 to 1932.
The Arab Medical Guide, Popular Health Organisations.
Directory to the schools in the Ottoman provinces,
Saliname, in Ottoman Turkish. Offices of General
Education, Istanbul, 1318 AH.
Two documents issued from the French civil records.
Municipality of Méru, in the Department of Oise, and
the Paris Municipality, 1911.

Death certificate. Records of the Latin community, Aleppo, 1918.

Certificate of Specialisation. College of Medicine, University of Paris, 23 May 1910 and 15 June 1911,

Golden Jubilee of the Faculty of Medicine, 1919–69. University of Damascus, 1969.

Magazine, *al-Umran*, special number about the history of Damascus and its drinking waters. Ain al-Fijja Water Authority, 1985.

University Certificate issued by the Faculty of Medicine, Istanbul, 1318 AH (AD 1902).

Manuscript notes for lectures, written in his own hand, given by Dr Rida Saïd, delivered to students specialising in ophthalmology at the Hôtel-Dieu, Paris, 1910.

ABOUT THE AUTHOR

Sabah Kabbani was born in the Shahm Minaret district of Damascus, 1928.

The house in which he was brought up was a centre for the national struggle. His well-known industrialist father, Tawfiq Kabbani, was a pillar of the Syrian campaign against the French Mandate, 1920–46.

After he completed his secondary education at the National Scientific College in Damascus he joined the Faculty of Law at the Syrian University and obtained a Diploma there in 1949.

He followed his higher studies in Paris where, in 1952, he obtained a Doctorate in International Law.

After he returned to his homeland he worked in the public sector between 1953 and 1981, when he resigned from official duties.

He worked in information, culture and diplomacy, including in the following posts.

Director of Programmes, Syrian Broadcasting, 1953

Director of Arts, Ministry of Culture, 1959, during the period of unity with Egypt.

Director of Television, 1960, during the period of union between Syria and Egypt.

Director of Television, 1963, after the restoration of national unity.

Consul-General for Syria in New York, 1962–66.

Director of Information, Ministry for Foreign Affairs, 1966–67.

Minister Plenipotentiary, Syrian Embassy, Jakarta, Indonesia, 1968–71.

Director of the American Department, Ministry for Foreign Affairs, 1972–74.

Ambassador, Syrian Embassy, Washington, DC, 1974–80.

Most of the tasks entrusted to him were innovative; he was one of the founders of Damascus broadcasting and of the Ministry of Culture; he was the founder and first Director of Syrian Television. Similarly he re-established the Embassy of the Syrian Arab Republic in Washington, DC when he was chosen as Syria's first Ambassador to the United States after the restoration of relations between the two countries in 1974.

Arising from his national commitment, in all the tasks he undertook inside and outside the country, he presented an enlightened picture of his country and his nation.

While he was working in the public sector, or alongside it, he was involved in various cultural and artistic activities. He wrote articles in Syrian, Arab and international newspapers, gave lectures in Syria and America, participated in television and radio discussions and undertook tasks for the

Ministry of Tourism, writing books in three languages – Arabic, French and English – presenting the cultural side of Syria. In addition he has many cultural interests, especially in photography. He has had several photography exhibitions, the most important of which was "Song of the Earth" in 1968, which portrayed aspects of beauty in the Syrian homeland.

WORKS BY THE AUTHOR

Translation from English of *Imperial Fictions: Europe's Myths of the Orient* by Rana Kabbani, published by Dar Tlass, Damascus, 1988

Translation from English of *Letter to Christendom* by Rana Kabbani, first printing, Dar al-Adab, Beirut, 1991; second printing, Dar al-Ahali, Damascus, 2000

Dimashq Nizar Qabbani, I'dadan wa Taswiran ("The Damascus of Nizar Kabbani, Arrangements and Illustrations"), Dar al-Ahali, Damascus, 1995

Min Awraq al-Umr ("From Documents of Life"), about his life in information, art and diplomacy, Dar al-Fikr, Damascus, 2008

Kalam ibr al-Ayyam ("Talk across the Ages"), writings on art, heritage and politics, Dar Tlass, Damascus, 2010

ABOUT THE TRANSLATOR

Peter Clark is a writer, translator and diarist. He worked for the British Council for over thirty years, including five years, 1992–97, in Syria. He has translated eight other books from Arabic, history and fiction, including two novels by Ulfat Idilbi. He was a Trustee of the Karim Rida Saïd Foundation from 1999 to 2004. His book, *Damascus Diaries, Life under the Assads*, was published in 2015, and he is also the author of *Churchill's Britain*, published in 2020. He is a Research Associate of the School of Oriental and African Studies, London.

The translator wishes to thank Mr Wafic Rida Saïd for his encouragement, support and advice, and Mr Hani Jesri for editorial support.

PRAISE FOR *RIDA SAÏD: A MAN FOR ALL SEASONS*

"The novelistic framework in which the writer places the life of Dr Rida Saïd produces a Greek hero struggling against his fates one after another. But for this dramatic framework that he has chosen, this book would not have differed from any other memoir. The author has clothed Dr Saïd with a cloak embroidered with culture that was not possible for anyone else. And fortunately he has the perceptive and creative eye to write about him."

The poet Nizar Kabbani, graduate of the Faculty of Law in the Syrian University, 1945

"I have read the book about Dr Rida Saïd as a story and been delighted; as a historical document I have learned much. It is beautiful and innovative at least in the writing of biography in our Arab literature. I believe it brings something quite new, and I hope that it will take its place in biographical literature and in narrative creativity."

The novelist Dr Abdul Salam al-Ujaili, graduate of the Faculty of Medicine in the Syrian University, 1945

"I have been much delighted by this book about Dr Rida Saïd. The novelistic style he uses will meet the approval of people today because it is far from the dry and document-based writing that is weary on the soul. The narrative language has its own fluency. The mass of information indicates the great pains the author has taken to achieve this effect."

Dr Marwan al-Hasini, former Professor in the Faculty of Medicine and President of the Arabic Language Academy; graduate of the Faculty of Medicine in the Syrian University, 1951

"I have enjoyed reading this book about our professor, Dr Rida Saïd, and discovered the author's golden pen and illuminating style that takes the reader along with the utmost pleasure and delight."

Dr (Ms) Izzat Muraidan, former Dean of the Faculty of Medicine, graduate of the School of Medicine in the Syrian University, 1930

"Many who have faced writing about that outstanding man Rida Saïd have hesitated, acknowledging their inadequacy. But the writer of this book has succeeded because he has approached the little information he has come across with the gifts of an artist and has written it in the form of a story to attract the reader. The author has discharged an obligation on behalf of us all to a man whose work is timeless and who worked for the benefit of generations. His life was a closed volume of memories that he has opened and published and from it has produced with delight and elegance a work that is an instructive pleasure for people."

Dr Burhan al-Abid, former Professor of the History of Medicine, graduate of the Faculty of Medicine in the Syrian University, 1950

"I have known Dr Rida Saïd and his family intimately. A close friendship linked me with them that extends for many years. But after I read this delightful memoir full of historical and documented detail, I can say that I have become more informed about the life of Dr Rida Saïd than I was before."

Ulfat al-Idilbi, Syrian writer